# The Student Lecture Companion:
## *A Note-Taking Guide to accompany Introduction to Java and Software Design*

by

**Nell Dale**
University of Texas, Austin

**Chip Weems**
University of Massachusetts, Amherst

**Mark Headington**
University of Wisconsin-La Crosse

Based on the PowerPoint presentation created
by
**Sylvia Sorkin**
Essex Community College

JONES AND BARTLETT PUBLISHERS
Sudbury, Massachusetts
BOSTON   TORONTO   LONDON   SINGAPORE

*World Headquarters*
Jones and Bartlett Publishers
40 Tall Pine Drive
Sudbury, MA 01776
978-443-5000
info@jbpub.com
www.jbpub.com

Jones and Bartlett Publishers Canada
2406 Nikanna Road
Mississauga, ON L5C 2W6
CANADA

Jones and Bartlett Publishers International
Barb House, Barb Mews
London W6 7PA
UK

Copyright © 2001 by Jones and Bartlett Publishers, Inc.

All rights reserved. No part of the material protected by this copyright notice may be reproduced or utilized in any form, electronic or mechanical, including photocopying, recording, or any information storage or retrieval system, without written permission from the copyright owner.

ISBN: 0-7637-1864-5

Printed in the United States of America
05 04 03 02 01   10 9 8 7 6 5 4 3 2 1

# Table of Contents

| | |
|---|---|
| How This Book Can Help You Learn Computer Science | vii |
| Note-Taking Tips | viii |
| Key Terms | ix-xiv |

## CHAPTER 1  Overview of Programming and Problem Solving — 1

**Chapter Topics**
- Computer Programming
- Programming Life-Cycle Phases
- Developing an Algorithm
- Machine Language vs. High Level Languages
- Compilation, Execution, and Interpretation
- Computer Components
- Computing Profession Ethics and Responsibilities
- Problem-Solving Techniques

## CHAPTER 2  Java Syntax and Semantics, and the Program Entry Process — 20

**Chapter Topics**
- Syntax Templates
- Data Types
- Java Identifiers
- Assignment Statements
- Declaring Named Constants and Variables
- String Concatenation
- Java Output Device `System.out`
- Two Java Comment Forms
- Debugging Process

## CHAPTER 3  Event-Driven Output — 32

**Chapter Topics**
- Packages `java.awt` and `java.awt.event`
- Importing a Package
- Declaring and Instantiating a Frame
- Invoking a Method
- Some Java History
- Using `GridLayout` Manager
- Registering an Event Listener
- Writing an Event Handler
- Using `WindowAdapter` Class

## CHAPTER 4  Numeric Types and Expressions                                43

**Chapter Topics**
Constants of Type `int` and `double`
Evaluating Arithmetic Expressions
Increment and Decrement Operators
Implicit Type Conversion and Explicit Type Casting
Calling a Value-Returning Method
Using Java `Math` Class Methods
String Operations `length`, `indexOf`, `substring`

## CHAPTER 5  Event-Driven Input and Software Design Strategies           69

**Chapter Topics**
Declaring and Instantiating a `TextField`
Declaring and Instantiating a `Button`
Handling `Button` Events with `actionPerformed`
Converting Strings into Numeric Types
Using the Object-Oriented Design (OOD) Strategy
Using CRC Cards
Using the Functional Decomposition Strategy
Using Pseudocode

## CHAPTER 6  Conditions, Logical Expressions, and Selection Control Structures   83

**Chapter Topics**
Java Control Structures
`boolean` Data Type
Using Relational and Logical Operators in Logical Expressions
`if-else` Selection Structure
`if` Selection Structure
Nested `if` Statements
Handling Multiple Button Events

## CHAPTER 7  Classes and Methods                                          110

**Chapter Topics**
Abstraction and Encapsulation in OOD
Designing the Public Interface for a Class
Designing a Class Constructor
Data Lifetime
Declaring Methods
Parameter Passing
Collecting Classes in a Package

## CHAPTER 8  Inheritance, Polymorphism, and Scope — 128
### Chapter Topics
- Inheritance and Class Hierarchy
- Overriding and Hiding
- Polymorphism
- Scope of Access Rules
- Method Signatures
- Method Overloading
- Keywords `super` and `this`
- Shallow Copy vs. Deep Copy of Objects
- Meaning of a Copy Constructor

## CHAPTER 9  File I/O and Looping — 141
### Chapter Topics
- Using Data Files for I/O
- While Statement Syntax
- Count-Controlled Loops
- Event-Controlled Loops
- Using the End-of-File Condition
- Using a While Statement for Summing and Counting
- Nested While Loops
- Loop Testing and Debugging

## CHAPTER 10  Additional Control Structures and Exceptions — 166
### Chapter Topics
- `switch` Multiway Branching Structure
- `do` Statement for Looping
- `for` Statement for Looping
- `break` Statement
- Bitwise Logical Operators
- Ternary and Assignment Operators
- Exception Handling using `try` and `catch`
- Defining Exception Classes

## CHAPTER 11  One-Dimensional Arrays — 186
### Chapter Topics
- Atomic and Composite Data Types
- Declaring and Instantiating an Array
- The Length of an Array
- Manipulating the Elements in an Array

Using an Array to Count Frequencies
Passing an Array to a Method

## CHAPTER 12  Array-Based Lists  198
**Chapter Topics**
Insertion and Deletion of List Items
Straight Selection Sort of List Items
Insertion and Deletion Using a Sorted List
Sequential Search for a List Item
Binary Search in a Sorted List
Order of Magnitude of a Function
Complexity of Searching and Sorting
Declaring and Using C Strings
Using the Java `Comparable` Interface

## CHAPTER 13  Multidimensional Arrays and Numeric Computation  216
**Chapter Topics**
Declaring and Using a Two-Dimensional Array
Two-Dimensional Arrays as Parameters
Returning Two-Dimensional Arrays from Methods
Ragged Arrays
Declaring and Using a Multidimensional Array

## CHAPTER 14  Recursion  228
**Chapter Topics**
Meaning of Recursion
Base Case and General Case in Recursive Definitions
Writing Recursive Algorithms with Simple Variables
Writing Recursive Algorithms with Structured Variables
Understanding How Recursion Works

# How This Book Can Help You Learn Computer Science

All of us have different learning styles. Some of us are visual learners, some more auditory, some learn better by doing an activity. Some students prefer to learn new material using visual aids. Some learn material better when they hear it in a lecture; others learn it better by reading it. Cognitive research has shown that no matter what your learning style, you will learn more if you are actively engaged in the learning process.

*The Student Lecture Companion* will help you learn by providing a structure to your notes and letting you utilize all of the learning styles mentioned above. Students don't need to copy down every word their professor says or recopy their entire Computer Science textbook. Do the assigned reading, listen in lecture, follow the key points your instructor is making, and write down meaningful notes. After reading and lectures, review your notes and pull out the most important points.

The *Student Lecture Companion* is your partner and guide in note-taking. Your *Companion* provides you with a visual guide that follows the chapter topics presented in your textbook, *Introduction to Java and Software Design*. The main topics covered in the lectures are listed in the Table of Contents. No more skimming through chapter after chapter trying to find the term you need to clarify! If your instructor is using the PowerPoint slides that accompany the text, this guide will save you from having to write down everything that is on the slides. There is space provided for you to jot down the terms and concepts that you feel are most important to each lecture. By working with your *Companion*, you are seeing, hearing, writing, and, later, reading and reviewing. The more times you are exposed to the material, the better you will learn and understand it. Using different methods of exposure significantly increases your comprehension.

Your *Companion* is the perfect place to write down questions that you want to ask your professor later, interesting ideas that you want to discuss with your study group, or reminders to yourself to go back and study a certain concept again to make sure that you really got it.

Having organized notes is essential at exam time, when doing homework assignments, or when working on programming problems. Your ability to easily locate the important concepts of a recent lecture will help you move along more rapidly, as you don't have to spend time rereading an entire chapter just to reinforce one point that you may not have quite understood.

Your *Companion* is a valuable resource. You've found a wonderful study partner!

# Note-Taking Tips

1. It is easier to take notes if you are not hearing the information for the first time. Read the chapter or the material that is about to be discussed before class. This will help you to anticipate what will be said in class, and have an idea of what to write down. It will also help to read over your notes from the last class. This way you can avoid having to spend the first few minutes of class trying to remember where you left off last time.

2. Don't waste your time trying to write down everything that your professor says. Instead, listen closely and only write down the important points. Review these important points after class to help remind you of related points that were made during the lecture.

3. If the class discussion takes a spontaneous turn, pay attention and participate in the discussion. Only take notes on the conclusions that are relevant to the lecture.

4. Emphasize main points in your notes. You may want to use a highlighter, special notation (asterisks, exclamation points), format (circle, underline), or placement on the page (indented, bulleted). You will find that when you try to recall these points, you will be able to actually picture them on the page.

5. Be sure to copy down word-for-word specific formulas, laws, and theories.

6. Hearing something repeated, stressed, or summed up can be a signal that it is an important concept to understand.

7. Organize handouts, study guides, and exams in your notebook along with your lecture notes. It may be helpful to use a three-ring binder, so that you can insert pages wherever you need to.

8. When taking notes, you might find it helpful to leave a wide margin on all four sides of the page. Doing this allows you to note names, dates, definitions, etc. for easy access and studying later. It may also be helpful to make notes of questions you want to ask your professor about or research later, ideas or relationships that you want explore more on your own, or concepts that you don't fully understand.

9. It is best to maintain a separate notebook for each class. Labeling and dating your notes can be helpful when you need to look up information from previous lectures.

10. Make your notes legible, and take notes directly in your notebook. Chances are you won't recopy them no matter how noble your intentions. Spend the time you would have spent recopying the notes studying them instead, drawing conclusions and making connections that you didn't have time for in class.

11. Look over your notes after class while the lecture is still fresh in your mind. Fix illegible items and clarify anything you don't understand. Do this again right before the next class.

# Key Terms

**Abstract data type**  A data type whose properties (domain and operations) are specified independently of any particular implementation.

**Abstract step**  A step for which some implementation details remain unspecified.

**Abstraction barrier**  The invisible wall around a class object that encapsulates implementation details. The wall can be breached only through the public interface.

**Aggregate operation**  An operation on a data structure as a whole, as opposed to an operation on an individual component of the data structure.

**Algorithm**  A stepbystep procedure for solving a problem in a finite amount of time.

**Anonymous type**  A type that does not have an associated type identifier.

**Argument**  A variable or expression listed in a call to a function; also called actual argument or actual parameter.

**Argument list**  A mechanism by which functions communicate with each other.

**Arithmetic/logic unit (ALU)**  The component of the central processing unit that performs arithmetic and logical operations.

**Array**  A collection of components, all of the same type, ordered on N dimensions (N ? 1). Each component is accessed by N indexes, each of which represents the component's position within that dimension.

**Assembler**  A program that translates an assembly language program into machine code.

**Assembly language**  A lowlevel programming language in which a mnemonic is used to represent each of the machine language instructions for a particular computer.

**Assignment expression**  A C++ expression with (1) a value and (2) the side effect of storing the expression value into a memory location.

**Assignment statement**  A statement that stores the value of an expression into a variable.

**Automatic variable**  A variable for which memory is allocated and deallocated when control enters and exits the block in which it is declared.

**Auxiliary storage device**  A device that stores data in encoded form outside the computer's main memory.

**Base address**  The memory address of the first element of an array.

**Base class (superclass)**  The class being inherited from.

**Binary operator**  An operator that has two operands.

**Black box**  An electrical or mechanical device whose inner workings are hidden from view.

**C string**  In C and C++, a null-terminated sequence of characters stored in a char array.

**Central processing unit (CPU)**  The part of the computer that executes the instructions (program) stored in memory; made up of the arithmetic/logic unit and the control unit.

**Class**  A structured type in a programming language that is used to represent an abstract data type.

**Class member**  A component of a class. Class members may be either data or functions.

**Class object (class instance)**  A variable of a class type.

**Client**  Software that declares and manipulates objects of a particular class.

**Communication complexity**  A measure of the quantity of data passing through a module's interface.

**Compiler**  A program that translates a highlevel language into machine code.

**Complexity** A measure of the effort expended by the computer in performing a computation, relative to the size of the computation.

**Composition (containment)** A mechanism by which the internal data (the state) of one class includes an object of another class.

**Computer** A programmable device that can store, retrieve, and process data.

**Computer program** A sequence of instructions to be performed by a computer.

**Computer programming** The process of planning a sequence of steps for a computer to follow.

**Concrete step** A step for which the implementation details are fully specified.

**Constructor** An operation that creates a new instance (variable) of an ADT.

**Control abstraction** The separation of the logical properties of an action from its implementation.

**Control structure** A statement used to alter the normally sequential flow of control.

**Control unit** The component of the central processing unit that controls the actions of the other components so that instructions (the program) are executed in the correct sequence.

**Countcontrolled loop** A loop that executes a specified number of times.

**Data** Information in a form a computer can use.

**Data abstraction** The separation of a data type's logical properties from its implementation.

**Data flow** The flow of information from the calling code to a function and from the function back to the calling code.

**Data representation** The concrete form of data used to represent the abstract values of an abstract data type.

**Data type** A specific set of data values, along with a set of operations on those values.

**Declaration** A statement that associates an identifier with a data object, a function, or a data type so that the programmer can refer to that item by name.

**Demotion (narrowing)** The conversion of a value from a "higher" type to a "lower" type according to a programming language's precedence of data types. Demotion may cause loss of information.

**Derived class (subclass)** The class that inherits.

**Documentation** The written text and comments that make a program easier for others to understand, use, and modify.

**Driver** A simple main function that is used to call a function being tested. The use of a driver permits direct control of the testing process.

**Dynamic binding** The run-time determination of which function to call for a particular object.

**Editor** An interactive program used to create and modify source programs or data.

**Encapsulation** Hiding a module implementation in a separate block with a formally specified interface.

**Enumeration type** A user-defined data type whose domain is an ordered set of literal values expressed as identifiers.

**Enumerator** One of the values in the domain of an enumeration type.

**Evaluate** To compute a new value by performing a specified set of operations on given values.

**Event counter** A variable that is incremented each time a particular event occurs.

**Eventcontrolled loop** A loop that terminates when something happens inside the loop body to signal that the loop should be exited.

**Expression** An arrangement of identifiers, literals, and operators that can be evaluated to compute a value of a given type.

**Expression statement** A statement formed by appending a semicolon to an expression.

**External representation**  The printable (character) form of a data value.

**Field (member, in C++)**  A component of a record.

**File**  A named area in secondary storage that is used to hold a collection of data; the collection of data itself.

**Flow of control**  The order in which the computer executes statements in a program.

**Function**  A subprogram in C++.

**Function call (function invocation)**  The mechanism that transfers control to a function.

**Function call (to a void function)**  A statement that transfers control to a void function. In C++, this statement is the name of the function, followed by a list of arguments.

**Function definition**  A function declaration that includes the body of the function.

**Function prototype**  A function declaration without the body of the function.

**Function value type**  The data type of the result value returned by a function.

**Functional cohesion**  A property of a module in which all concrete steps are directed toward solving just one problem, and any significant subproblems are written as abstract steps.

**Functional cohesion**  The principle that a module should perform exactly one abstract action.

**Functional decomposition**  A technique for developing software in which the problem is divided into more easily handled subproblems, the solutions of which create a solution to the overall problem.

**Functional equivalence**  A property of a module that performs exactly the same operation as the abstract step it defines. A pair of modules are also functionally equivalent to each other when they perform exactly the same operation.

**Hardware**  The physical components of a computer.

**Hierarchical record**  A record in which at least one of the components is itself a record.

**Identifier**  A name associated with a function or data object and used to refer to that function or data object.

**Information**  Any knowledge that can be communicated.

**Information hiding**  The encapsulation and hiding of implementation details to keep the user of an abstraction from depending on or incorrectly manipulating these details.

**Inheritance**  A mechanism by which one class acquires the properties-the data and operations-of another class.

**Input/output (I/O) devices**  The parts of the computer that accept data to be processed (input) and present the results of that processing (output).

**Interactive system**  A system that allows direct communication between user and computer.

**Interface**  A connecting link at a shared boundary that allows independent systems to meet and act on or communicate with each other.

**Interface**  A connecting link at a shared boundary that permits independent systems to meet and act on or communicate with each other. Also, the formal description of the purpose of a subprogram and the mechanism for communicating with it.

**Internal representation**  The form in which a data value is stored inside the memory unit.

**Iteration**  An individual pass through, or repetition of, the body of a loop.

**Iteration counter**  A counter variable that is incremented with each iteration of a loop.

**Iterator**  An operation that allows us to process-one at a time-all the components in an instance of an ADT.

**Length**  The number of values currently stored in a list.

**Lifetime**  The period of time during program execution when an identifier has memory allocated to it.

**List** A variable-length, linear collection of homogeneous components.

**Literal value** Any constant value written in a program.

**Local variable** A variable declared within a block and not accessible outside of that block.

**Loop** A control structure that causes a statement or group of statements to be executed repeatedly.

**Loop entry** The point at which the flow of control reaches the first statement inside a loop.

**Loop exit** The point at which the repetition of the loop body ends and control passes to the first statement following the loop.

**Loop test** The point at which the While expression is evaluated and the decision is made either to begin a new iteration or skip to the statement immediately following the loop.

**Machine language** The language, made up of binarycoded instructions, that is used directly by the computer.

**Member selector** The expression used to access components of a struct variable. It is formed by using the struct variable name and the member name, separated by a dot (period).

**Memory unit** Internal data storage in a computer.

**Metalanguage** A language that is used to write the syntax rules for another language.

**Mixed type expression** An expression that contains operands of different data types; also called mixed mode expression.

**Module** A selfcontained collection of steps that solves a problem or subproblem; can contain both concrete and abstract steps.

**Name precedence** The precedence that a local identifier in a function has over a global identifier with the same name in any references that the function makes to that identifier; also called name hiding.

**Named constant (symbolic constant)** A location in memory, referenced by an identifier, that contains a data value that cannot be changed.

**Named type** A user-defined type whose declaration includes a type identifier that gives a name to the type.

**Nonlocal identifier** With respect to a given block, any identifier declared outside that block.

**Object program** The machine language version of a source program.

**Object-oriented design** A technique for developing software in which the solution is expressed in terms of objects-self-contained entities composed of data and operations on that data.

**Object-oriented programming (OOP)** The use of data abstraction, inheritance, and dynamic binding to construct programs that are collections of interacting objects.

**Observer** An operation that allows us to observe the state of an instance of an ADT without changing it.

**Onedimensional array** A structured collection of components, all of the same type, that is given a single name. Each component (array element) is accessed by an index that indicates the component's position within the collection.

**Operating system** A set of programs that manages all of the computer's resources.

**Out-of-bounds array index** An index value that, in C++, is either less than 0 or greater than the array size minus 1.

**Parameter** A variable declared in a function heading; also called formal argument or formal parameter.

**Peripheral device** An input, output, or auxiliary storage device attached to a computer.

**Polymorphic operation** An operation that has multiple meanings depending on the type of the object to which it is bound at run time.

**Postcondition** An assertion that should be true after a module has executed.

**Precision** The maximum number of significant digits.

**Precondition** An assertion that must be true before a module begins executing.

**Programming**  Planning or scheduling the performance of a task or an event.

**Programming language**  A set of rules, symbols, and special words used to construct a computer program.

**Promotion (widening)**  The conversion of a value from a "lower" type to a "higher" type according to a programming language's precedence of data types.

**Range of values**  The interval within which values of a numeric type must fall, specified in terms of the largest and smallest allowable values.

**Record (structure, in C++)**  A structured data type with a fixed number of components that are accessed by name. The components may be heterogeneous (of different types).

**Reference parameter**  A parameter that receives the location (memory address) of the caller's argument.

**Representational error**  Arithmetic error that occurs when the precision of the true result of an arithmetic operation is greater than the precision of the machine.

**Reserved word**  A word that has special meaning in C++; it cannot be used as a programmer-defined identifier.

**Scope**  The region of program code where it is legal to reference (use) an identifier.

**Scope rules**  The rules that determine where in the program an identifier may be accessed, given the point where that identifier is declared.

**Selfdocumenting code**  Program code containing meaningful identifiers as well as judiciously used clarifying comments.

**Semantics**  The set of rules that determines the meaning of instructions written in a programming language.

**Short-circuit (conditional) evaluation**  Evaluation of a logical expression in left-to-right order with evaluation stopping as soon as the final truth value can be determined.

**Side effect**  Any effect of one function on another that is not a part of the explicitly defined interface between them.

**Significant digits**  Those digits from the first nonzero digit on the left to the last nonzero digit on the right (plus any 0 digits that are exact).

**Simple (atomic) data type**  A data type in which each value is atomic (indivisible).

**Software**  Computer programs; the set of all programs available on a computer.

**Software engineering**  The application of traditional engineering methodologies and techniques to the development of software.

**Software piracy**  The unauthorized copying of software for either personal use or use by others.

**Sorting**  Arranging the components of a list into order (for instance, words into alphabetical order or numbers into ascending or descending order).

**Source program**  A program written in a highlevel programming language.

**Static binding**  The compile-time determination of which function to call for a particular object.

**Static variable**  A variable for which memory remains allocated throughout the execution of the entire program.

**Structured (procedural) programming**  The construction of programs that are collections of interacting functions or procedures.

**Structured data type**  A data type in which each value is a collection of components and whose organization is characterized by the method used to access individual components. The allowable operations on a structured data type include the storage and retrieval of individual components.

**Stub**  A dummy function that assists in testing part of a program. A stub has the same name and interface as a function that actually would be called by the part of the program being tested, but it is usually much simpler.

**Switch expression**  The expression whose value determines which switch label is selected. It cannot be a floating-point or string expression.

**Syntax** The formal rules governing how valid instructions are written in a programming language.

**Termination condition** The condition that causes a loop to be exited.

**Test plan** A document that specifies how a program is to be tested.

**Test plan implementation** Using the test cases specified in a test plan to verify that a program outputs the predicted results.

**Testing the state of a stream** The act of using a C++ stream object in a logical expression as if it were a Boolean variable; the result is true if the last I/O operation on that stream succeeded, and false otherwise.

**Transformer** An operation that builds a new value of the ADT, given one or more previous values of the type.

**Twodimensional array** A collection of components, all of the same type, structured in two dimensions. Each component is accessed by a pair of indexes that represent the component's position in each dimension.

**Type casting** The explicit conversion of a value from one data type to another; also called type conversion.

**Type coercion** The implicit (automatic) conversion of a value from one data type to another.

**Unary operator** An operator that has just one operand.

**Value parameter** A parameter that receives a copy of the value of the corresponding argument.

**Value-returning function** A function that returns a single value to its caller and is invoked from within an expression.

**Variable** A location in memory, referenced by an identifier, that contains a data value that can be changed.

**Virus** A computer program that replicates itself, often with the goal of spreading to other computers without authorization, and possibly with the intent of doing harm.

**Void function (procedure)** A function that does not return a function value to its caller and is invoked as a separate statement.

# Introduction to Java and Software Design

## Dale • Weems • Headington

Copyright © 2001 Jones and Bartlett Publishers

 This project was supported in part by the National Science Foundation under award DUE-ATE 9950056. Opinions are those of the authors and do not necessarily reflect the views of the National Science Foundation.

*Slides by Sylvia Sorkin, The Community College of Baltimore County – Essex Campus*

# Chapter 1: Overview of Programming and Problem Solving

**Notes**

### Introduction to Java and Software Design

Dale • Weems • Headington

Chapter 1

Overview of Programming and Problem Solving

### Chapter 1 Topics

- Computer Programming
- Programming Life-Cycle Phases
- Developing an Algorithm
- Machine Language vs. High Level Languages
- Compilation, Execution and Interpretation
- Computer Components
- Computing Profession Ethics and Responsibilities
- Problem-Solving Techniques

### What is Computer Programming?

- It is the process of specifying the data types and the operations for a computer to apply to data in order to solve a problem.

  STEP 1
  STEP 2
  STEP 3
  . . .

## Programming Life Cycle Phases

1. Problem-Solving

2. Implementation

3. Maintenance

## Problem-Solving Phase

- ANALYZE the problem and SPECIFY what the solution must do.

- Develop a GENERAL SOLUTION (ALGORITHM) to solve the problem.

- VERIFY that your solution really solves the problem.

## Sample Problem

- A programmer needs an algorithm to determine an employee's weekly wages.

- How would the calculations be done by hand?

**Notes**

**Notes**

### One Employee's Wages

- During one week an employee works 52 hours at the hourly pay rate $24.75
- How much are the employee's wages?
- Assume a 40.0 hour normal work week.
- Assume an overtime pay rate factor of 1.5

| 40 x $24.75 | = $ 990.00 |
|---|---|
| 12 x 1.5 x $24.75 | = $ 445.50 |
| | $ 1435.50 |

### Weekly Wages, in General

If hours is over 40.0, then

   wages = (40.0 * payRate) + (hours - 40.0) * 1.5 * payRate

**RECALL EXAMPLE**
( 40 x $24.75 ) + ( 12 x 1.5 x $24.75 ) = **$1435.50**

otherwise,

   wages = hours * payRate

### An Algorithm is . . .

- step-by-step instructions for solving a problem in a finite amount of time using a finite amount of data.

## Algorithm to Determine an Employee's Weekly Wages

1. Get the employee's hourly pay rate
2. Get the hours worked this week
3. Calculate this week's regular wages
4. Calculate this week's overtime wages (if any)
5. Add the regular wages to overtime wages (if any) to determine total wages for the week

## What is a Programming Language?

- It is a language with strict grammatical rules, symbols, and special words used to construct a computer program.

## Implementation Phase: Program

- Translating your algorithm into a programming language is called CODING.

- With Java, you use

    Documentation -- your written comments

    Compiler -- translates your program into Bytecode

    Java Virtual Machine -- translates Bytecode into machine language

## Notes

### Implementation Phase: Test

- TESTING your program means executing (running) your program on the computer, to see if it produces correct results.

- If it does not, then you must find out what is wrong with your program or algorithm and fix it. This is called debugging.

### Maintenance Phase

- USE and MODIFY the program to meet changing requirements or correct errors that show up in using it.

- Maintenance begins when your program is put into use and accounts for the majority of effort on most programs.

### Programming Life Cycle

1 **Problem-Solving**
   Analysis and Specification
   General Solution ( Algorithm )
   Verify

2 **Implementation**
   Concrete Solution ( Program )
   Test

3 **Maintenance**
   Use
   Maintain

## Programming Shortcut?

PROBLEM-SOLVING PHASE
- Problem → Algorithm

IMPLEMENTATION PHASE
- Shortcut? ✗ → Code
- Algorithm → Code

## Binary Representation of Data

- Circuit states correspond to 0 and 1.
- Bit (short for binary digit) refers to a single 0 or 1. Bit patterns represent data.
- 1 byte = 8 bits
- 1 KB = 1024 bytes
- 1 MB = 1024 x 1024 = 1,048,576 bytes

## How Many Possible Digits?

- Binary (Base 2) Numbers use 2 digits:
  JUST 0 and 1

- Decimal (Base 10) Numbers use 10 digits:
  0 THROUGH 9

**Notes**

**Notes**

### Machine Language

- Is not portable
- Runs only on specific type of computer
- Is made up of binary-coded instructions (strings of 0s and 1s)
- Is the language that can be directly used by the computer.

### Assembly Language

- Is machine dependent. Compilers translate assembly language into machine language.
- Runs only on specific type of computer.
- Is made up of English-like abbreviations like LOAD, STORE, ADD.

### High Level Languages

- Are portable. Generally compilers translate high-level language into machine language.
- User writes program in language similar to natural language.
- Examples -- FORTRAN, COBOL, Pascal, C, C++
- Many are standardized by ISO/ANSI to provide an official description of the language.

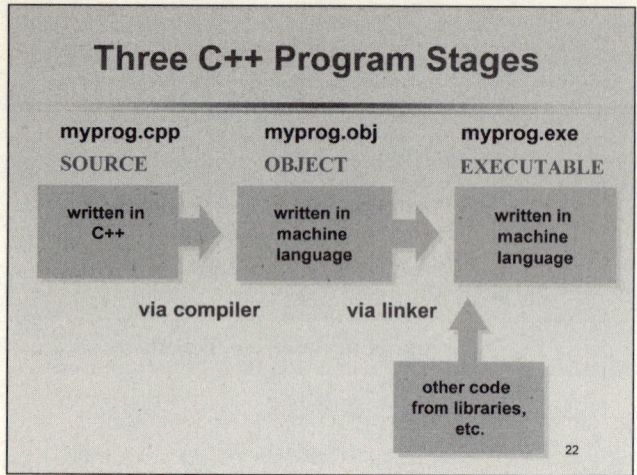

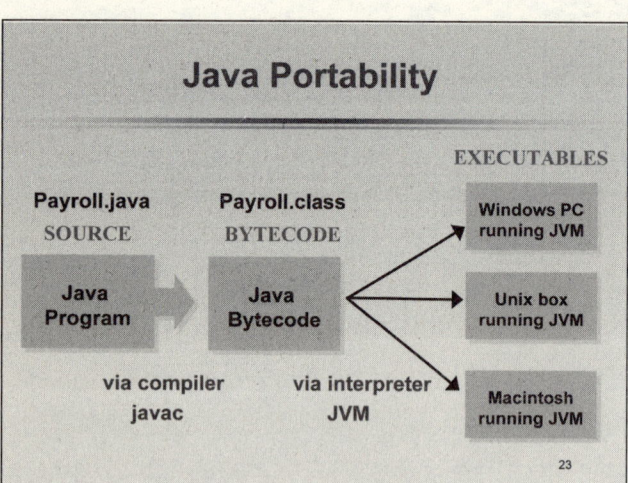

## Java programming language

- Achieves portability by using both a compiler and an interpreter.
- First, a Java compiler translates a Java program into an intermediate Bytecode--not machine language.
- Then, an interpreter program called the Java Virtual Machine (JVM) translates a single instruction in the Bytecode program to machine language and immediately runs it, one at a time.

**Notes**

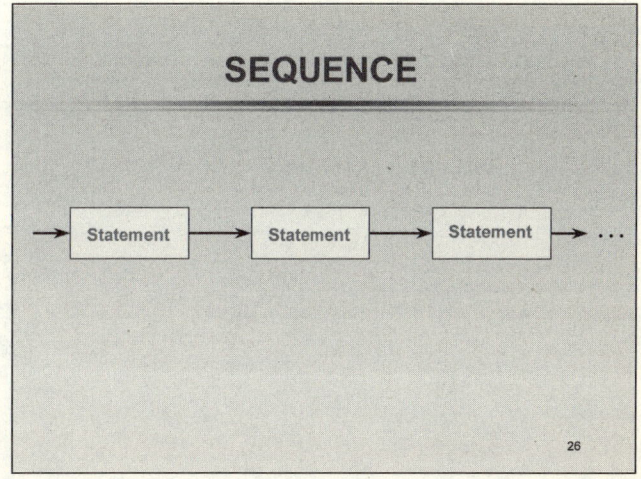

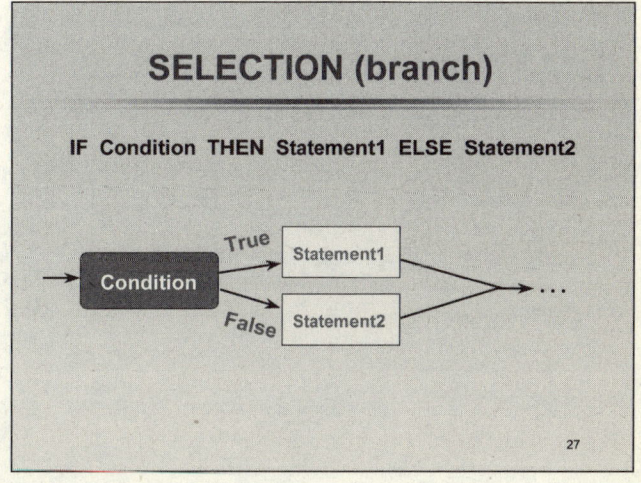

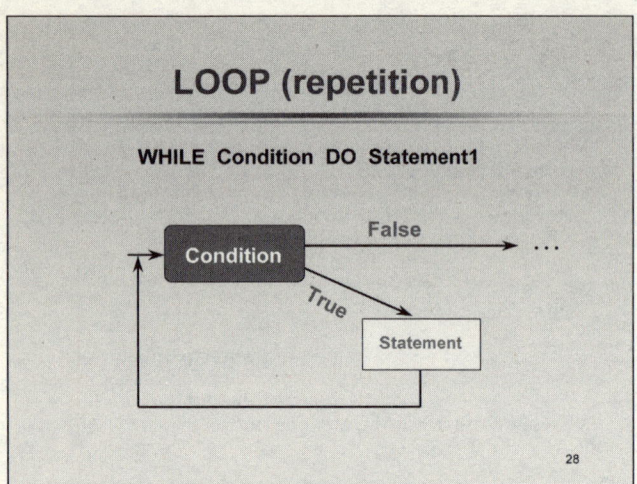

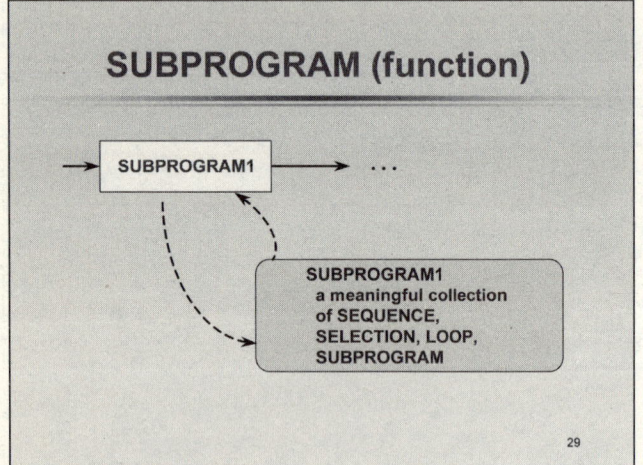

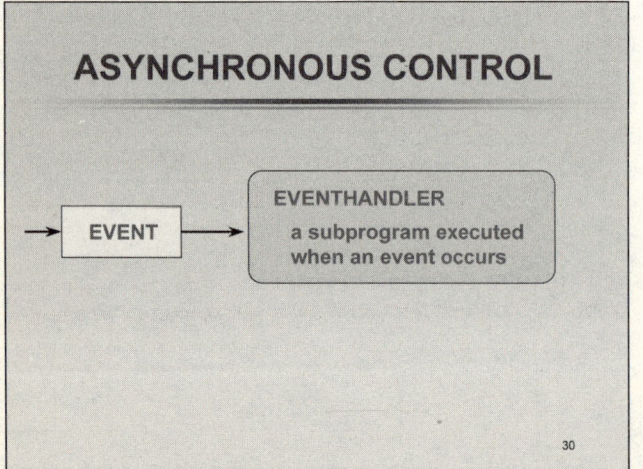

**Notes**

## Notes

### Object-Oriented Programming

- An object is a collection of data values and associated operations.

- A class is a description of one or more like objects.

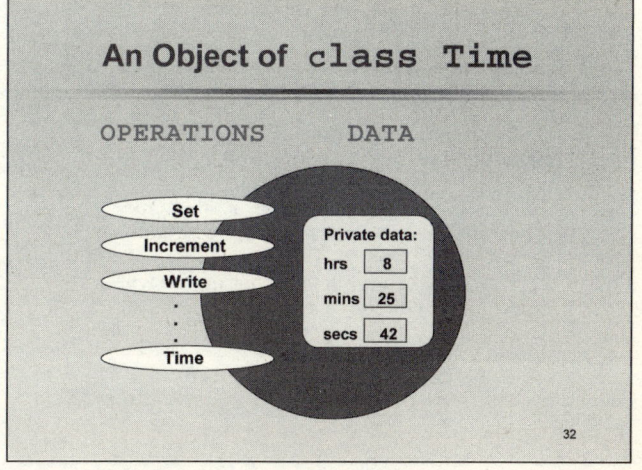

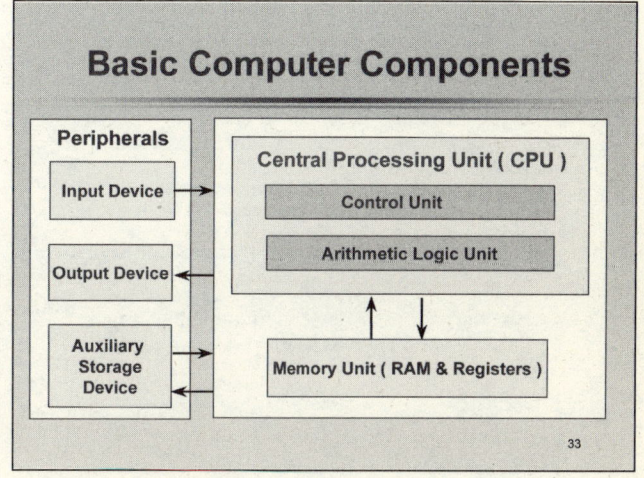

## Memory Unit

- Is an ordered sequence of storage cells, each capable of holding a piece of data.
- Each memory cell has a distinct address.
- The information held can be input data, computed values, or program instructions.

## Central Processing Unit (CPU)

- Has 2 components to execute program instructions --
    - Arithmetic/Logic Unit performs arithmetic operations, and makes logical operations.
    - Control Unit controls the order in which your program instructions are executed.

## Peripheral Devices

- Are input, output, or auxiliary storage devices attached to a computer.
    - Input Devices include keyboard and mouse.
    - Output Devices include printers, video display, LCD screens.
    - Auxiliary Storage Devices include disk drives, CD-ROM and DVD-ROM drives.

**Notes**

**Notes**

### Computing Profession Ethics

- Copy software only with permission from the copyright holder.
- Give credit to another programmer by name whenever using his/her code.
- Use computer resources only with permission.
- Guard the privacy of confidential data.
- Use software engineering principles to develop software free from errors.

### Problem Solving Techniques

- ASK QUESTIONS -- about the data, the process, the output, error conditions.
- LOOK FOR FAMILIAR THINGS -- certain situations arise again and again.
- SOLVE BY ANALOGY -- it may give you a place to start.
- USE MEANS-ENDS ANALYSIS -- Determine the I/O and then work out the details.

### More Problem Solving Techniques

- DIVIDE AND CONQUER -- break up large problems into manageable units.
- BUILDING-BLOCK APPPROACH -- can you solve small pieces of the problem?
- MERGE SOLUTIONS -- instead of joining them end to end to avoid duplicate steps.
- OVERCOME MENTAL BLOCK -- by rewriting the problem in your own words.

## Company Payroll Case Study

- A company needs a program to figure its weekly payroll.
- The file datafile.dat contains each employee's identification number, pay rate, and hours worked.
- Each employee's data and calculated wages should be saved in a file, payfile.dat
- Display the total wages for the week on the screen.

## One Employee's Wages

- During one week employee # 458759761 works 52 hours at the hourly pay rate $24.75
- How much are the employee's wages?
- Assume a 40.0 hour normal work week.
- Assume an overtime pay rate factor of 1.5

| | |
|---|---|
| 40 x $ 24.75 = | $  990.00 |
| 12 x 1.5 x $ 24.75 = | $  445.50 |
| | $ 1435.50 |

## Problem-Solving Phase

Processing each employee's data in turn --

INPUT DATA for employee from datafile

COMPUTED VALUE of wages

OUTPUT RESULTS to screen

**Notes**

# Notes

## Problem-Solving Phase

**INPUT DATA**
- Employee ID Number
- Hourly payRate
- Hours worked

**FORMULA CONSTANTS**
- Normal work hours (40.0)
- Overtime pay rate factor (1.5)

**OUTPUT RESULTS**
- Hourly payRate
- Hours worked
- Wages

**COMPUTED VALUE**
- Wages

## Week's Wages, in General

If hours worked is over 40.0, then

wages = (40.0 * payRate) + (hours - 40.0) * 1.5 *payRate

**RECALL EXAMPLE**
( 40 x $ 24.75 ) + ( 12 x 1.5 x $ 24.75 ) = $1435.50

otherwise

wages = hours * payRate

## Company Payroll Algorithm

Prepare to read employee information from file
Prepare to write employee wages to file
Initialize total company payroll to 0.0
While these is more data on datafile.dat
    Read employee number
    Read hourly pay rate
    Read hours worked
    Calculate wages
    Add wages to total company payroll
    Write employee information and wages to file
Write total company payroll in window on screen.

**Notes**

```java
// Company Payroll program

import java.awt.*;
import java.awt.event.*;
import java.io.*;

public class Payroll
{
  private static Frame outputDisplay;    // Declare Frame

  static double calcPay(double payRate, double hours)

  //  calcPay computes wages from employee's pay rate
  //  and hours worked, taking overtime into account

  {
      final double MAX_HOURS = 40.0;
      final double OVERTIME = 1.5;
      if (hours > MAX_HOURS)
         return (MAX_HOURS * payRate) +
                (hours - MAX_HOURS) * payRate * OVERTIME;
      else
         return hours * payRate;
  }
```
46

```java
   public static void main( String[ ] args )
          throws IOException, NumberFormatException

// main is where execution starts.  It opens 2 files,
// and processes the data file.  Then shows the total in a
// Frame on screen and exits when user closes the window.
   {
       String    empNum;          // Employee's ID
       double    payRate;         // Employee's pay rate
       double    hours;           // Hours worked
       double    wages;           // Wages earned
       double    total = 0.0;     // Total company payroll

       BufferedReader  dataFile;  // File for input
       PrintWriter     payFile;   // File for printing

       // Open company payroll files

       dataFile = new BufferedReader(
                   new FileReader("datafile.dat"));

       payFile = new PrintWriter(
                   new FileWriter("payfile.dat"));
```
47

```java
       empNum = dataFile.readLine( );      // Read ID

       while ( empNum != null )            // While not done
       {
          payRate = Double.valueOf(
                    dataFile.readLine( ) ).doubleValue( );
                                           // Read pay rate
          hours = Double.valueOf(
                    dataFile.readLine( ) ).doubleValue( );
                                           // Read hours

          wages = CalcPay(payRate, hours); // Compute wages

          total = total + wages;           // Add wages to total

          payFile.println( empNum + " " + payRate + " " +
                           hours + " " + wages );

          empNum = dataFile.readLine( );   // Read next ID
       }
```
48

# Notes

```
dataFile.close( );          // Close input file
payFile.close( );           // Close output file

// Create a Frame and display it on screen
outputDisplay = new Frame( );

// Specify layout manager for frame
outputDisplay.setLayout( new FlowLayout( ) );

outputDisplay.add( new Label
        ("Total payroll for the week is $" + total));

outputDisplay.add( new Label
        ("Close window to exit program."));

outputDisplay.pack( );
outputDisplay.show( );
```

## Creating a WindowAdapter

```
// Event handler for window closing

outDisplay.addWindowListener( new WindowAdapter( )

// Create a WindowAdapter
    {
        // Method to handle event
        public void windowClosing (WindowEvent event)
        {
            outputDisplay.dispose( );  // Remove frame
            System.exit( 0 );          // Quit program
        }
    });
}
}
```

## class WindowAdapter

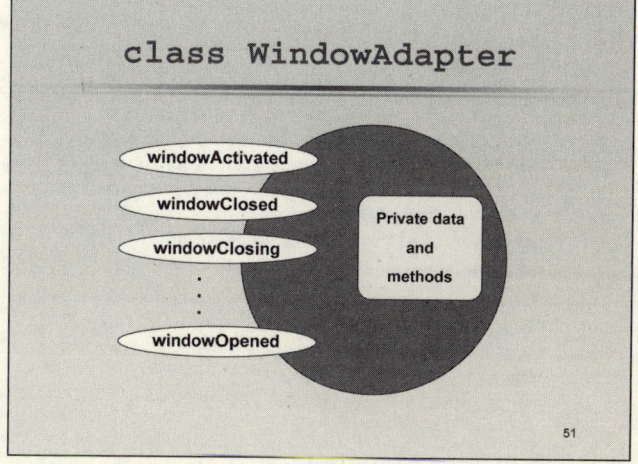

## Input file `datafile.dat`

```
534923445
6.54
45
103428439
12.82
38
131909545
8.20
52
739219803
10.00
40
```

## Output file `payfile.dat`

```
534923445  6.54  45.0  310.65000000000003
103428439  12.82  38.0  487.16
131909545  8.2  52.0  475.6
739219803  10.0  40.0  400.0
```

## Two Types of Java Programs

**APPLETS** can be loaded from a remote computer into the web browser, executed in the browser, and discarded when execution completes. An HTML document refers to the applet. Such browsers have the Java Virtual Machine (JVM) interpreter built into the browser.

**APPLICATIONS** are normally stored on the user's local computer and executed using the JVM interpreter.

**Notes**

## Some Java History

- 1991 -- James Gosling at Sun Microsystems began development
- 1993 -- Potential of using Java to create Web pages with dynamic content
- 1995 -- Sun formally announced Java
- Java Developer's Kit (JDK) available free from Sun® at
    http://www.javasoft.com/products

## Some JDK Tools

- javac -- Java compiler compiles .java files and produces Java bytecode (.class) files that can be executed by any Java Virtual Machine (JVM) interpreter on any platform.

- java -- Java Virtual Machine (JVM) interpreter loads .class files and executes Java program.

## Executing Java Applications

- The application source file name must be the same as the class name and end with .java
- Java applications must have a method main with first line heading

```
public static void main( String[ ] args )
```

- To compile the Java application with Sun's javac compiler enter at DOS prompt
    
    javac Payroll.java

- To execute Java application with Sun's JVM interpreter enter at DOS prompt
    
    java Payroll

# Chapter 2: Java Syntax and Semantics, and the Program Entry Process

## Introduction to Java and Software Design

Dale • Weems • Headington

Chapter 2
Java Syntax and Semantics,
and the Program Entry Process

## Chapter 2 Topics

- Syntax Templates
- Data Types
- Java Identifiers
- Assignment Statements
- Declaring Named Constants and Variables
- String Concatenation
- Java Output Device `System.out`
- Two Java Comment Forms
- Debugging Process

## What is syntax?

- **Syntax** is a formal set of rules that defines exactly what combinations of letters, numbers, and symbols can be used in a programming language.
- Syntax rules are written in a simple, precise formal language called a metalanguage.
- Some metalanguages are Backus-Naur-Form, syntax diagram, and syntax template.

# Notes

### Identifier Syntax Template

- Blue shading indicates an optional part of the definition. Three dots . . . mean the preceding symbol or shaded block can be repeated. A word not in color can be replaced with another template.

**Identifier**

[ Letter / _ / $ ] [ Letter / _ / Digit / $ ] . . .

**Letter**: A B C D E F G H I J K L M N O P Q R S T U V W X Y Z  a b c d e f g h i j k l m n o p q r s t u v w x y z

**Digit**: 0 1 2 3 4 5 6 7 8 9

### Java Identifiers

- A Java identifier must start with a letter or underscore or dollar sign, and be followed by zero or more letters (A-Z, a-z), digits (0-9), underscores, or dollar signs.

**VALID**

age_of_dog          taxRateY2K
HourlyEmployee      ageOfDog

**NOT VALID (Why?)**

age#      2000TaxRate      Age-Of-Dog

The Student Lecture Companion

## What is an Identifier?

- An *identifier* is the name used for a class, method (subprogram), field (a variable or a named constant), or package in a Java program.
- Java is a *case-sensitive* language.
- Using meaningful identifiers is a good programming practice.

## 51 Java Reserved Words

| | | | | |
|---|---|---|---|---|
| abstract | boolean | break | byte | case |
| catch | char | class | const | continue |
| default | do | double | else | extends |
| false | final | finally | float | for |
| goto | if | implements | import | instanceof |
| int | interface | long | native | new |
| null | package | private | protected | public |
| return | short | static | strictfp | super |
| switch | synchronized | this | throw | throws |
| transient | true | try | void | volatile |
| while | | | | |

Reserved words cannot be used as identifiers.

## Samples of Java Data Values

int sample values
    4578        -4578        0

double sample values
    95.274      95.        .265

char sample values
    'B'    'd'    '4'    '?'    '*'

**Notes**

## ASCII and Unicode

- ASCII (pronounced ask-key) is an older character set used to represent characters internally as integers.
- ASCII is a subset of the newer Unicode character set.
- Using ASCII the character 'A' is internally stored as integer 65. In both sets, the successive alphabet letters are stored as successive integers. This enables character comparisons with 'A' less than 'B', etc.

## Primitive Data Types in Java

- **Integral Types**
  - can represent whole numbers and their negatives when declared as int, short, or long
  - can represent single characters when declared as char

- **Floating Point Types**
  - represent real numbers with a decimal point
  - declared as float, or double

## Java Primitive Data Types

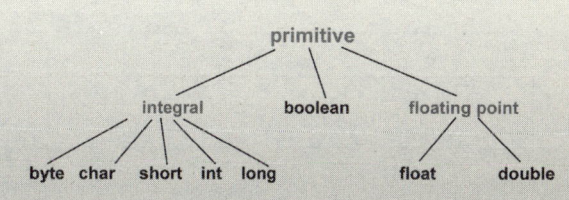

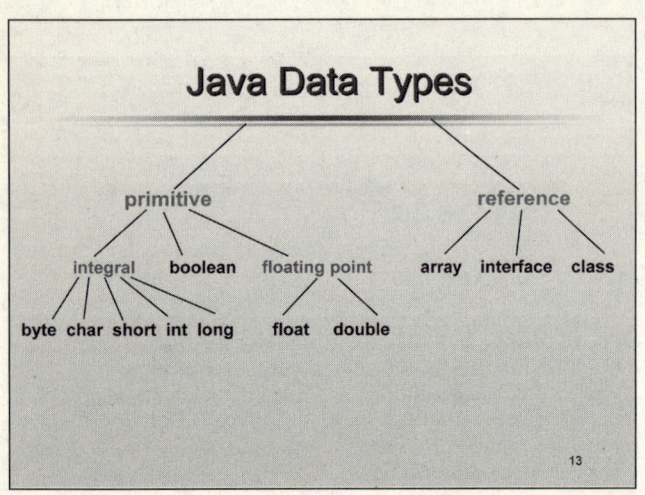

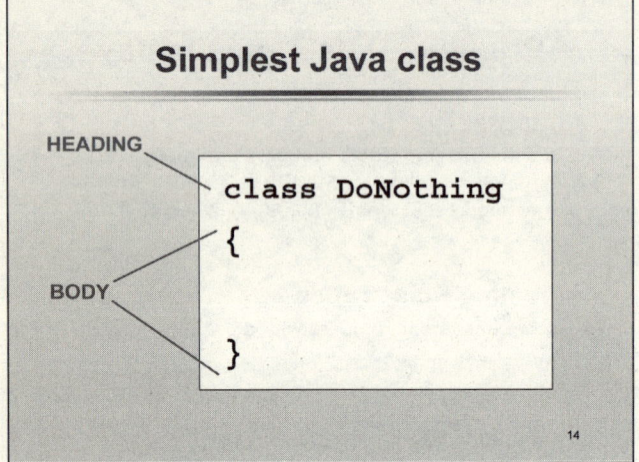

**Notes**

**Notes**

## Block (Compound Statement)

- A block is a sequence of zero or more statements enclosed by a pair of curly braces { }.

**Block**

```
{
        Statement
        . . .
}
```

## What is a Variable?

- A variable is a location in memory which we can refer to by an identifier, and in which a data value that can be changed is stored.

- Declaring a variable means specifying both its name and its data type or class.

## What Does a Variable Declaration Do?

```
int     ageOfDog;
```

A declaration tells the compiler to allocate enough memory to hold a value of this data type, and to associate the identifier with this location.

4 bytes for ageOfDog

## Syntax for Declarations

**Variable Declaration**

Modifiers  TypeName  Identifier , Identifier . . . ;

**Constant Declaration**

Modifiers  final TypeName  Identifier = LiteralValue ;

## Java data type String

- A string is a sequence of characters enclosed in double quotes.
- string sample values
  ```
  "Today and tomorrow"
  "His age is 23."
  ```
- The empty string contains no characters and is written as  `""`

## Java's String class

- String operations include
  - joining one string to another (concatenation)
  - converting number values to strings
  - converting strings to number values
  - comparing 2 strings

**Notes**

### What is a Named Constant?

- A **named constant** is a location in memory which we can refer to by an identifier, and in which a **data value that cannot be changed** is stored.

VALID NAMED CONSTANT DECLARATIONS

```
final   String   STARS       =  "****" ;
final   float    NORMAL_TEMP =  98.6 ;
final   char     BLANK       =  ' ' ;
final   int      VOTING_AGE  =  18 ;
final   double   MAX_HOURS   =  40.0 ;
```

### Giving a value to a variable

You can assign (give) a value to a variable by using the assignment operator =

**VARIABLE DECLARATIONS**

```
String  firstName ;
char    middleInitial ;
char    letter ;
int     ageOfDog;
```

**VALID ASSIGNMENT STATEMENTS**

```
firstName = "Fido" ;
middleInitial = 'X' ;
letter = middleInitial ;
ageOfDog = 12 ;
```

### Assignment Statement Syntax

Variable = Expression ;

First, Expression on right is evaluated.

Then the resulting value is stored in the memory location of Variable on left.

NOTE: The value assigned to Variable must be of the same type as Variable.

The Student Lecture Companion

## String concatenation (+)

- Concatenation uses the + operator.

- A built-in type value can be concatenated with a string because Java automatically converts the built-in type value for you to a string first.

## Concatenation Example

```
final   int   DATE = 2001;
final   String   phrase1 = "Introduction to Java and ";
final   String   phrase2 = "Software Design ";
String bookTitle;

bookTitle = phrase1 + phrase2;
System.out.println(bookTitle + " has copyright " + DATE);
```

## Using Java output device

**METHOD CALL SYNTAX**

**System.out.print ( *StringValue* ) ;**
**System.out.println ( *StringValue* ) ;**

These examples yield the same output.

```
System.out.print( "The answer is, " ) ;
System.out.println( "Yes and No." ) ;
```

```
System.out.println( "The answer is, Yes and No." ) ;
```

**Notes**

## Notes

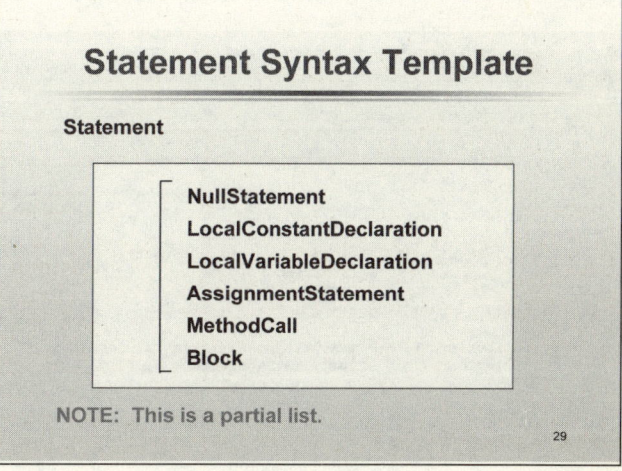

## Java Program

```java
// ****************************************************
// PrintName program
// This program prints a name in two different formats
// ****************************************************
public class PrintName
{
  public static void main (String[ ] args)
  {
    final  string  FIRST  = "Herman";     // Person's first name
    final  string  LAST   = "Herrmann";   // Person's last name
    final  char    MIDDLE = 'G';          // Person's middle initial
```

## Java program continued

```java
    String    firstLast;   // Name in first-last format
    String    lastFirst;   // Name in last-first format

    firstLast = FIRST + " " + LAST ;

    System.out.println( "Name in first-last format is "
                         + firstLast );

    lastFirst = LAST + ", " + FIRST + ", " ;

    System.out.println( "Name in last-first-intial format is "
                         + lastFirst + MIDDLE + "." );
  }
}
```

## Output displayed on screen

Name in first-last format is Herman Hermann
Name in last-first-initial format is Herrmann, Herman, G.

# Notes

### One Form of Java Comments

- Comments between /* and */ can extend over several lines.

```
/* This is a Java comment.  It can extend over more
   than one line.  */

/* In this second Java comment the asterisk on the next line
 * is part of the comment itself.
 */
```

### Another Form of Java Comment

- Using two slashes // makes the rest of the line become a comment.

```
// **********************************************************
// PrintName program
// This program prints a name in two different formats
// **********************************************************

final  String  FIRST  = "Herman";   // Person's first name
final  char    MIDDLE = 'G';        // Person's middle initial
```

### Debugging Process

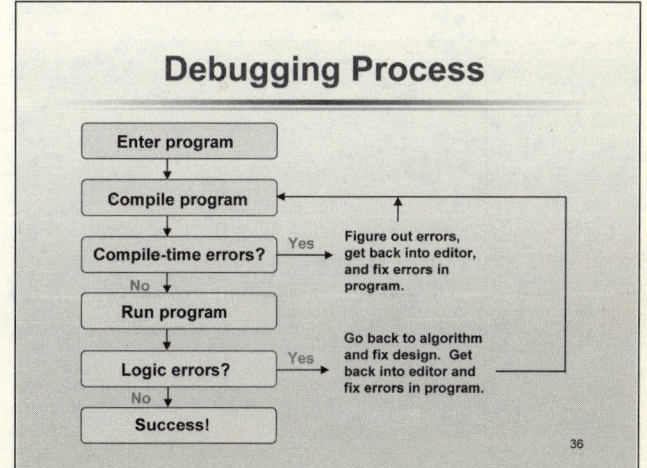

# Chapter 3: Event-Driven Output

### Introduction to Java and Software Design

Dale • Weems • Headington

Chapter 3

Event-Driven Output

### Chapter 3 Topics

- Packages `java.awt` and `java.awt.event`
- Importing a Package
- Declaring and Instantiating a `Frame`
- Invoking a Method
- Some Java History
- Using `GridLayout` Manager
- Registering an Event Listener
- Writing an Event Handler
- Using `WindowAdapter` class

### Interface

An interface is a **connecting link at a shared boundary** that allows independent systems to meet and act on or communicate with each other.

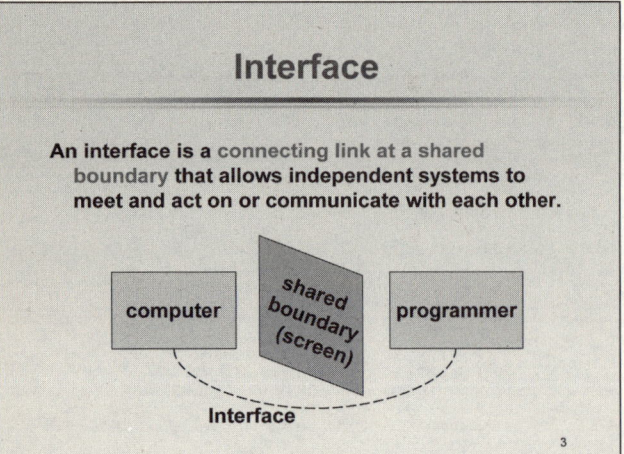

**Notes**

# Notes

## Event-Driven Programming

- Java uses event-driven programming. The user's interaction with a GUI component is an event that can be processed by the program.

- To do so, a GUI component (such as a Frame) is told using a method (such as `addWindowListener`) where the event-handling method is defined that will be called when an event involving that component occurs.

## Steps for using an output Frame

1. Import packages from library
2. Declare a Frame variable
3. Use new to instantiate the Frame object
4. Specify a layout manager for the Frame
5. Add output to the Frame (such as a Label)
6. Pack the Frame (adjust size to fit)
7. Show the Frame on the screen

## Using an output Frame

```
import java.awt.*;                      // Import package
. . .
private static Frame outputDisplay;     // Declare Frame variable
. . .
outputDisplay = new Frame( );           // Instantiate outputDisplay

                                        // Specify layout manager for frame
outputDisplay.setLayout( new FlowLayout( ) );

outputDisplay.add( new Label("Total is $" + total));

outputDisplay.pack( );
outputDisplay.show( );
```

**Notes**

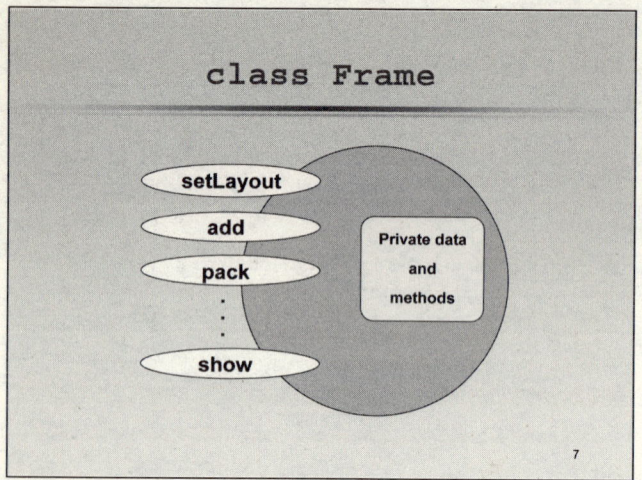

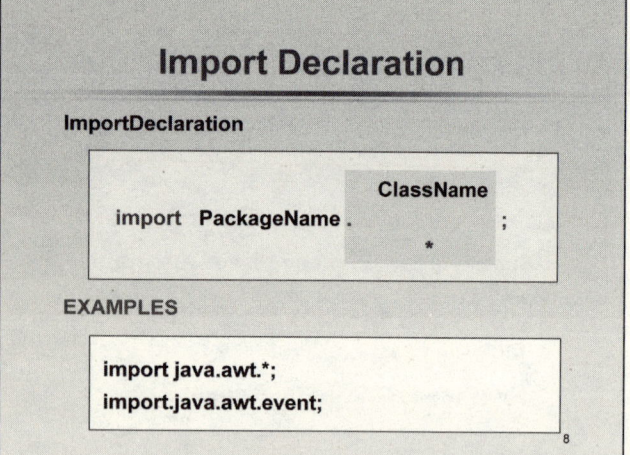

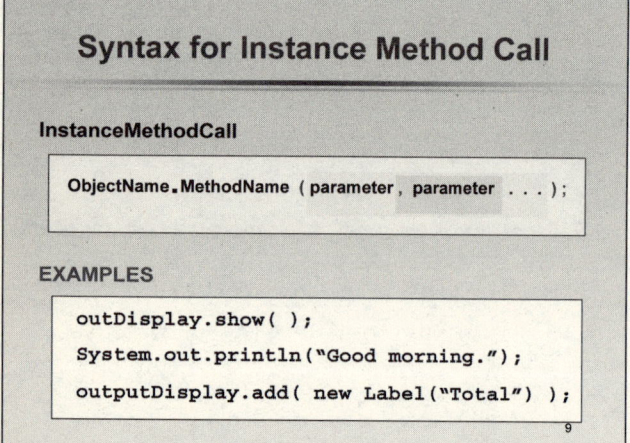

# Notes

## Class Constructors

- A **constructor is a class method** whose name must be the same as the class containing it.
- A class may have several constructors with different parameter lists. A constructor with no parameters is the **default** constructor.
- A constructor is **automatically called** whenever a new object of that class is created (using operator **new**). The purpose of the constructor is to provide information used to instantiate the new object.

## Some of the `java.awt` Hierarchy

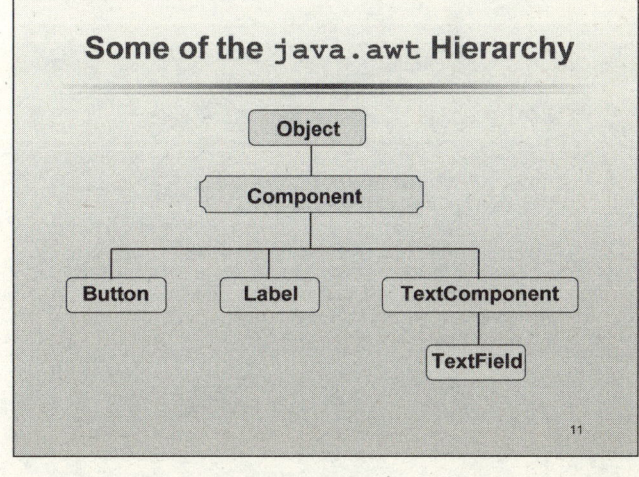

## class Label constructors

```
//   Constructors
public Label( )
//   Constructs a Label with no text displayed

public Label( String s )
//   Constructs a Label with text s aligned left-justified

public Label( String s, int alignment )
//   Constructs a Label with text s and specified alignment
//   such as Label.LEFT, Label.CENTER, or Label.RIGHT
```

## More of the `java.awt` Hierarchy

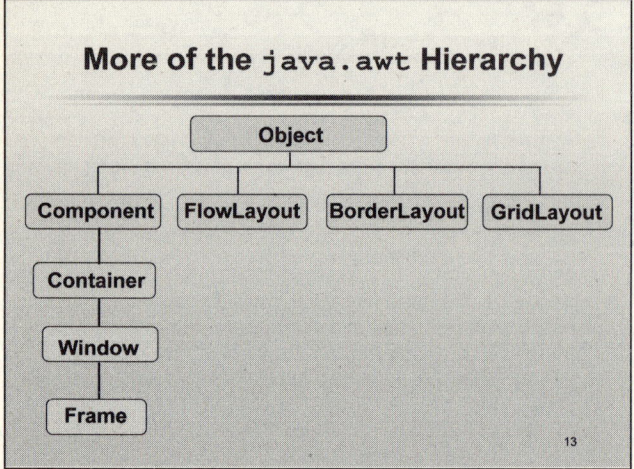

## Some Java History

- 1991 -- James Gosling at Sun Microsystems began development
- 1993 -- Potential of using Java to create Web pages with dynamic content
- 1995 -- Sun formally announced Java
- Java Developer's Kit (JDK) available free from Sun® at
    http://www.javasoft.com/products

## Some GUI components

| | |
|---|---|
| `Frame` | A kind of window in which components can be placed. |
| `Label` | A component where text can be displayed. |
| `Button` | A component that generates an event when the user clicks on it with the mouse. |
| `TextField` | A component in which the user can type a value. The user must first place the cursor in the field by clicking inside the field. |

**Notes**

**Notes**

### Graphical User Interfaces

- GUIs are built from GUI components (also called widgets for window gadgets).
- GUI component classes are part of java.awt (Abstract Windowing Toolkit package).
- GUIs are event-driven. They generate events when the user interacts with the GUI.
- An event is an action such as clicking the mouse, clicking a button, that takes place asynchronously (not at a particular time) with respect to the execution of the program.

### Closing a Frame

- Clicking the close window box generates an asynchronous window event. It can occur at any time.
- Clicking the close window box at the top of a Frame will not actually close that window unless you provide a WindowListener for the Frame with a method named windowClosing.

### 2 Steps for processing an event

- Register an event listener object to "listen" for specific types of events.
- Implement event handler method(s) to be called automatically in response to a particular type of event.
- A class that implements an event listener interface must provide a definition for every method of that interface.

## Delegation event model

- **Means** the use of event listeners in event handling.
- **The processing of an event is delegated to a particular object in the program.**
- **Using** a separate class to define an event listener is a common practice **for separating the GUI interface from the implementation of its event handler.**

## Handling a window event

- `Window` objects (including `Frame` objects) generate "window events" that can be processed by any `WindowListener` object.
- Any class that implements interface WindowListener must provide a definition for seven methods (including windowClosing).
- Once a WindowListener object is registered to "handle" an action event, these seven methods are called automatically whenever a window event occurs.

## Two of the event-listener interfaces in package `java.awt.event`

```
              java.util.EventListener
                       |
          ┌────────────┴────────────┐
   WindowListener              ActionListener
```

## Notes

## Adapter Classes

- If a program needs only a few handler methods from an event-listener interface, there are adapter classes that provide empty bodies for each method in the corresponding interface.
- One of these adapter classes is WindowAdapter.
- The advantage of using an adapter class in your program is that you can then just define whatever method(s) you actually need for event handling.

## class WindowAdapter

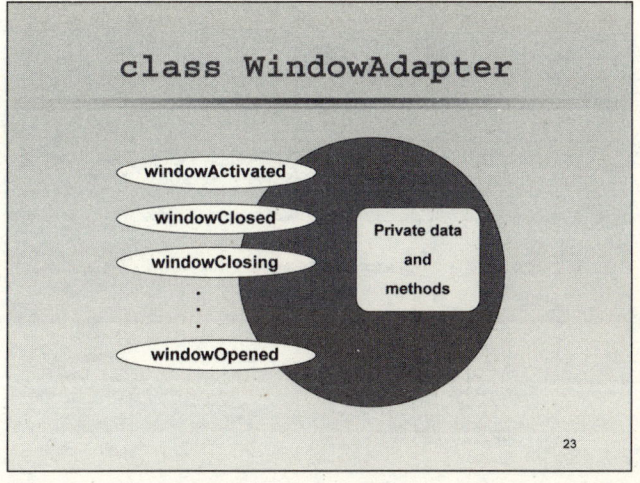

## Layout Managers

| | |
|---|---|
| FlowLayout | Default manager for Frames. Places components one after another in the order they were added. |
| GridLayout | Partitions the Frame into a fixed number of rows and columns. Successively fills the grid cells one row at a time. |

## FlowLayout constructor

```
// Constructor

public FlowLayout( )
// Constructs a FlowLayout with components center aligned
```

EXAMPLE

```
outputDisplay.setLayout( new FlowLayout( ) );
```

## Using GridLayout

```
payRoll.setLayout( new GridLayout( 4, 2 ) );
```

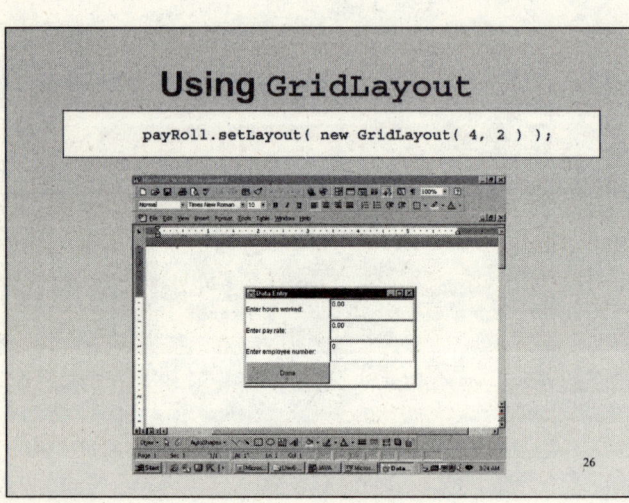

## GridLayout constructor

```
// Constructor
// In GridLayout, components are put in rows as added.

public GridLayout( int rows, int columns )
   // Constructs a GridLayout with specified number of
   // rows and columns, with all columns of equal size.
   // Using 0 for rows enables you to have an arbitrary
   // number of rows.  Using 0 for columns enables GridLayout
   // to provide any number of columns, all the size of the
   // largest component.
```

# Notes

## DateFormats Program

```
// *********************************************************
// DateFormats program
// Prints a date in four formats using concatenation.
// *********************************************************
import   java.awt.*;           // Import Frame type, etc.
import   java.awt.event.*;     // Import event handling types
public class DateFormats
{
  private static Frame outputDisplay;    // Declare Frame

  public static void main( String[ ] args )
  {
     final String   MONTH_NAME = "August"; // name of month
     final String   MONTH_NUMBER = "8";    // number of month
     final String   DAY = "17";            // day of month
     final String   YEAR = "2001";         // 4-digit year
```

```
     String   first;       // Date in Month day, year form
     String   second;      // Date in day Month year format
     String   third;       // Date in mm/dd/yyyy format
     String   fourth;      // Date in dd/mm/yyyy format

     // Instantiate a Frame object
     outputDisplay = new Frame( );
     outputDisplay.setLayout( new GridLayout(5, 2) );

     // Set up headings
     outputDisplay.add( new Label("Format"));
     outputDisplay.add( new Label("Example"));

     // Add information to the screen
     outputDisplay.add( new Label("Month day, year"));
     first = MONTH_NAME + " " + DAY + ", " + + YEAR;
     outputDisplay.add( new Label(first) );
```

```
     // Add more information to the screen
     outputDisplay.add( new Label("day Month year"));
     second = DAY + " " + MONTH_NAME + " " + + YEAR;
     outputDisplay.add( new Label(second) );

     outputDisplay.add( new Label("mm/dd/yyyy"));
     third = MONTH_NUMBER + "/" + DAY + "/" + YEAR;
     outputDisplay.add( new Label(third) );

     outputDisplay.add( new Label("dd/mm/yyyy"));
     fourth = DAY + "/" + MONTH_NUMBER + "/" + + YEAR;
     outputDisplay.add( new Label(fourth) );

     outputDisplay.pack( );
     outputDisplay.show( );
```

### Creating a `WindowAdapter`

```
    // Event handler for window closing
    outDisplay.addWindowListener( new WindowAdapter( )

    // Create a WindowAdapter
    {
        // Method to replace the empty one
        public void windowClosing (WindowEvent event)
        {
            outputDisplay.dispose( );   // Remove frame
            System.exit( 0 );           // Quit program
        }
    });
  }
}
```

**Notes**

# Chapter 4: Numeric Types and Expressions

**Notes**

## Introduction to Java and Software Design

Dale • Weems • Headington

Chapter 4

Numeric Types and Expressions

## Chapter 4 Topics

- Constants of Type `int` and `double`
- Evaluating Arithmetic Expressions
- Increment and Decrement Operators
- Implicit Type Conversion and Explicit Type Casting
- Calling a Value-Returning Method
- Using Java `Math` class methods
- `String` Operations `length`, `indexOf`, `substring`

## Java Primitive Data Types

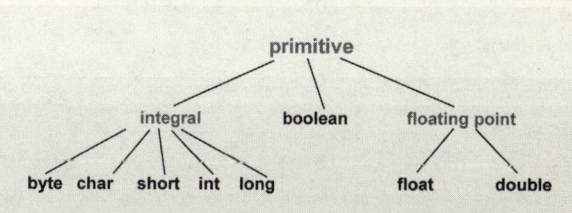

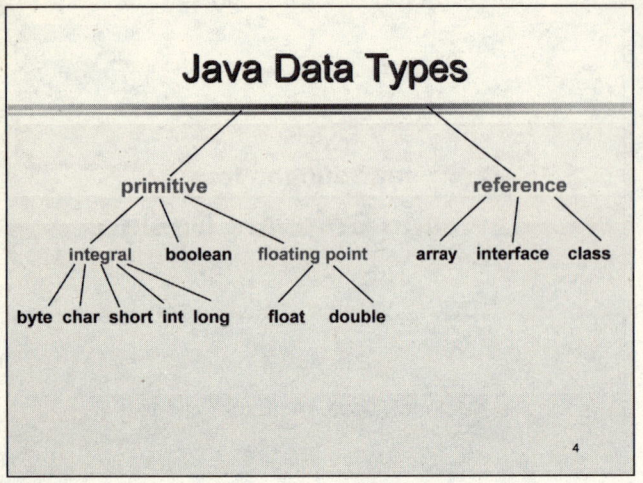

**Notes**

## Primitive and Reference Types

```
char letter ;
String title ;
String book ;
letter = 'J' ;
title = "Software Design";
book = title ;
```

letter [　　]
title  [　　]
book   [　　]

## Primitive and Reference Types

```
char letter ;
String title ;
String book ;
letter = 'J' ;
title = "Software Design";
book = title ;
```

letter [ 'J' ]
title  [　　]
book   [　　]

## Primitive and Reference Types

```
char letter ;
String title ;
String book ;
letter = 'J' ;
title = "Software Design";
book = title ;
```

Memory Location 2000 → "Software Design"

letter [ 'J' ]
title  [ 2000 ]
book   [　　]

## Primitive and Reference Types

```
char letter ;
String title ;
String book ;
letter = 'J' ;
title = "Software Design";
book = title ;
```

Memory Location 2000

"Software Design"

letter  'J'
title  2000
book  2000

## Primitive and Reference Types

```
char letter ;
String title ;
String book ;
letter = 'J' ;
title = "Software Design";
book = title ;
```

Memory Location 2000

"Software Design"

letter  'J'
title  2000
book  2000

## Primitive Data Types in Java

**Integral Types**
- can represent whole numbers and their negatives when declared as short, int, or long
- can represent single characters when declared as char

**Floating Point Types**
- represent real numbers with a decimal point
- declared as float, or double

**Notes**

### Samples of Java Data Values

int sample values
 4578        -4578        0

double sample values
 95.274      95.         .265

char sample values
 'B'   'd'   '4'   '?'   '*'

### Exponential (Scientific) Notation

2.7E4 means $2.7 \times 10^4$ =
2.7000 =
27000.0

2.7E-4 means $2.7 \times 10^{-4}$ =
0002.7 =
0.00027

### More About Floating Point Types

- Floating-point types have an integer part and a fractional part, with a decimal point in between. Either the integer part or the fractional part, but not both, may be missing.

**EXAMPLES**    18.4    500.    .8    -127.358

- Alternatively, floating point values can have an exponent, as in scientific notation. The number preceding the letter E doesn't need to include a decimal point.

**EXAMPLES**    1.84E1    5E2    8E-1    -.127358E3

The Student Lecture Companion

## What is an Arithmetic Expression?

- An arithmetic expression is a valid arrangement of variables, constants, operators and parentheses.

- An expression can be evaluated to compute a value of a given type.

- The value of the expression
  9.3 * 4.5  is  41.85

## Division Operator

- **The result of the division operator depends on the type of its operands.**

- **If one or both operands has a floating type, the result is a floating point type (float or double). Otherwise, the result is an integral type.**

**EXAMPLES**

```
11 / 4       has value   2
11.0 / 4.0   has value   2.75
11 / 4.0     has value   2.75
```

```java
// ****************************************************
// FreezeBoil   program
// This program computes the midpoint between
// the freezing and boiling points of water
// ****************************************************
import java.awt.*;
import java.awt.event.*;
public class FreezeBoil
{
  private static Frame out;

  public static void main( String[ ] args )
  {
      final double FREEZE_PT = 32.0;   // Freezing point
      final double BOIL_PT = 212.0;    // Boiling point

      double avgTemp;       // Holds result of averaging
                            // FREEZE_PT and BOIL_PT
```

# Notes

```
out = new Frame( );           // Create new frame
                              // Specify layout manager
out.setLayout( new FlowLayout( ) );

out.add( new Label ("Water freezes at "
                  + FREEZE_PT ) );

out.add( new Label ("and boils at "
                  + BOIL_PT + " degrees.") );
avgTemp = FREEZE_PT + BOIL_PT ;
avgTemp = avgTemp / 2.0 ;

out.add( new Label("Halfway between is "
                  + avgTemp + " degrees.") );

out.pack( );                  // Pack the frame
out.show( );                  // Show frame on screen
```

## Creating a WindowAdapter

```
// Event handler for window closing

out.addWindowListener( new WindowAdapter( )

// Create a WindowClosing method
    {
        // Method to handle event
        public void windowClosing (WindowEvent event)
        {
            out.dispose( );         // Remove frame
            System.exit(0);         // Quit program
        }
    });
}
```

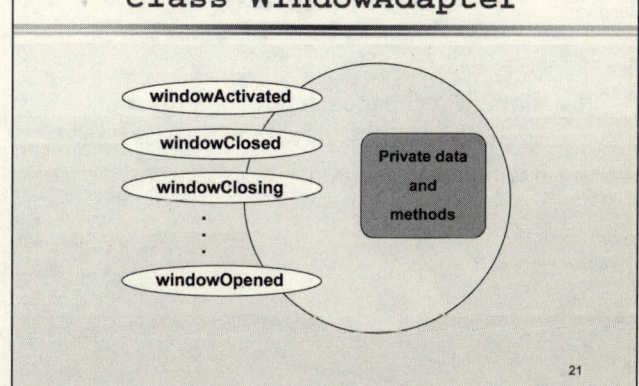

## Modulus Operator

- The modulus operator % when used with integer type operands has an integer type result.
- Its result is the integer type remainder of an integer division.

EXAMPLE

11 % 4 has value 3 because

2 and Remainder = ?
4 ) 11

## Some Java Operators

| Precedence | Operator | Description |
|---|---|---|
| Higher | ( ) | Parentheses |
| | + | Positive |
| | - | Negative |
| | * | Multiplication |
| | / | Division |
| | % | Modulus (remainder) |
| | + | Addition |
| | - | Subtraction |
| Lower | = | Assignment |

## Precedence

- **Higher Precedence** determines which operator is applied first in an expression having several operators.

**Notes**

## Associativity

- Left to right Associativity means that in an expression having 2 operators with the same priority, the left operator is applied first.

- In Java, the binary operators
    *, /, %, +, - are all left associative.

```
Expression  9 - 5 - 1  means  ( 9 - 5 ) - 1
                                   4 - 1
                                     3
```

## Evaluate the Expression

```
              7 * 10 - 5 % 3 * 4 + 9
      means  (7 * 10) - 5 % 3 * 4 + 9
              70 - 5 % 3 * 4 + 9
              70 - (5 % 3) * 4 + 9
              70 -   2 * 4 + 9
              70 - ( 2 * 4) + 9
              70 - 8 + 9
             ( 70 - 8 ) + 9
               62   + 9
                  71
```

## Parentheses

- Parentheses can be used to change the usual order.
- Parts in ( ) are evaluated first.
- Evaluate   (7 * (10 - 5) % 3) * 4 + 9
             ( 7 * 5 % 3 ) * 4 + 9
             ( 35 % 3 ) * 4 + 9
                  2 * 4 + 9
                    8 + 9
                     17

## More Java Operators

```
int age;

age = 8;

age = age + 1;
```

8
age

9
age

## PREFIX FORM
## Increment Operator

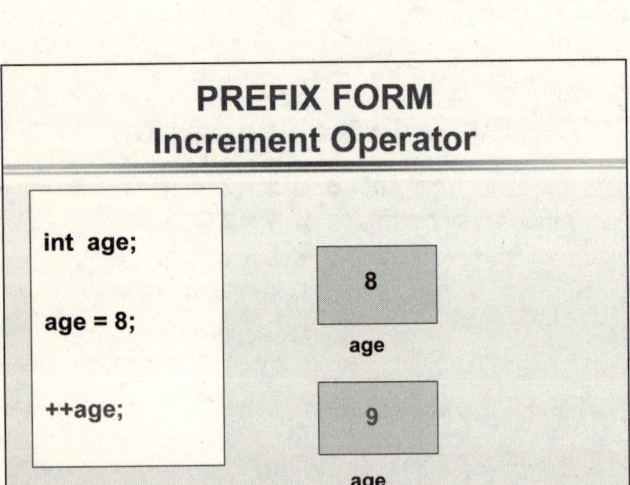

```
int age;

age = 8;

++age;
```

## POSTFIX FORM
## Increment Operator

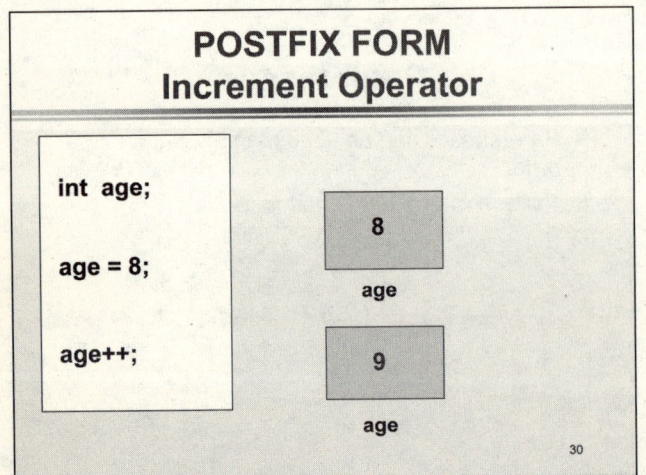

```
int age;

age = 8;

age++;
```

## Notes

### Decrement Operator

```
int  dogs;

dogs = 100;

dogs--;
```

100
dogs

99
dogs

### Which form to use?

- When the increment (or decrement) operator is used in a *"stand alone" statement* solely to add one (or subtract one) from a variable's value, it can be used in either prefix or postfix form.

USE EITHER

dogs-- ;          --dogs;

### BUT...

- When the increment (or decrement) operator is used in a statement with other operators, the prefix and postfix forms can yield *different* results.

LET'S SEE HOW...

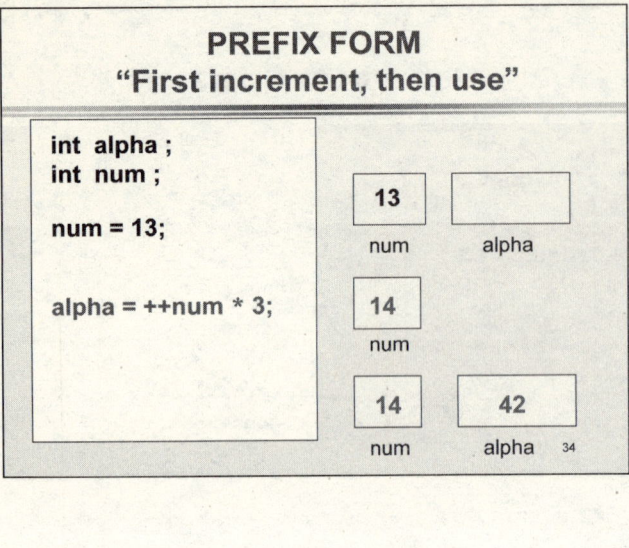

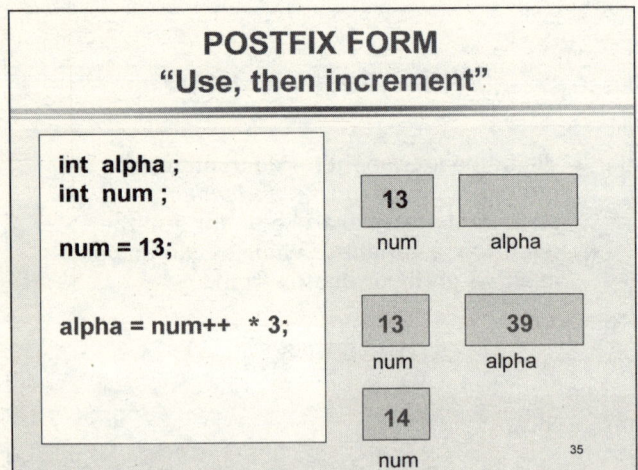

## Integral Types

| Type | Size in Bits | Minimum Value to Maximum Value |
|---|---|---|
| byte | 8 | -128 to 127 |
| short | 16 | -32,768 to 32,767 |
| int | 32 | -2,147,483,648 to 2,147,483,647 |
| long | 64 | -9,223,372,036,854,775,808 to +9,223,372,036,854,775,807 |

**Notes**

# Notes

## Sizes of Integral Java Types

byte    8 bits

short   16 bits

int     32 bits

long    64 bits

## Using one byte ( = 8 bits ),

| 0 | 1 | 1 | 0 | 0 | 0 | 1 | 1 |

**HOW MANY DIFFERENT NUMBERS CAN BE REPRESENTED USING 0's and 1's?**

Each bit can hold either a 0 or a 1. So there are just two choices for each bit, and there are 8 bits.

$$2 \times 2 \times 2 \times 2 \times 2 \times 2 \times 2 \times 2 = 2^8 = 256$$

## Similarly, using two bytes ( = 16 bits ),

| 0 | 1 | 1 | 0 | 0 | 0 | 1 | 1 | 0 | 1 | 0 | 0 | 1 | 0 | 1 | 0 |

$$2^{16} = 65536$$

**DIFFERENT NUMBERS CAN BE REPRESENTED.**

If we wish to have only one number representing the integer zero, and half of the remaining numbers positive, and half negative, we can obtain the 65,536 numbers in the range below:

$$-32768 \ldots 0 \ldots 32767$$

The Student Lecture Companion

## More about Floating-Point Types

- In Java floating-point literals like 94.6 without a suffix are of type double by default.

- To obtain another floating point type constant a suffix must be used.

- The suffix F or f denotes float type, as in 94.6F

## Floating Point Types

| Type | Size in Bits | Range of Values |
|------|--------------|-----------------|
| float | 32 | ±1.4E-45 to ±3.4028235E+38 |
| double | 64 | ±4.9E-324 to ±1.7976931348623157E+308 |

## Assignment Operator Syntax

Variable = Expression

First, Expression on right is evaluated.

Then the resulting value is stored in the memory location of Variable on left.

NOTE: An automatic type conversion occurs after evaluation but before the value is stored if the types differ for Expression and Variable

# Notes

## What value is stored?

```
double a;
double b;

a = 8.5;
b = 9.37;
a = b;
```

| a | 8.5  |      | a | ? |
|---|------|------|---|---|
| b | 9.37 | →    | b | ? |

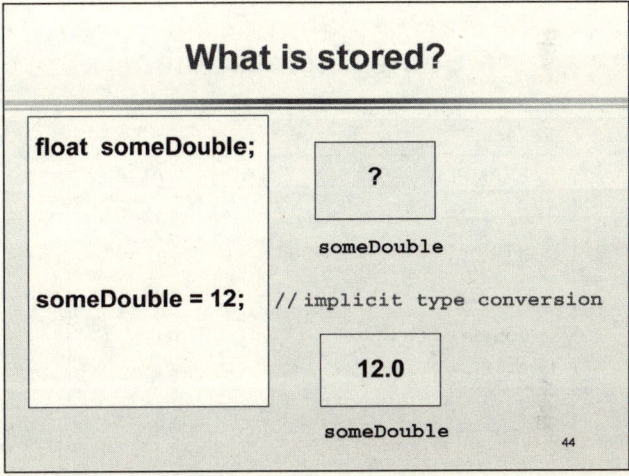

## What is stored?

```
float someDouble;

someDouble = 12;
```

// implicit type conversion

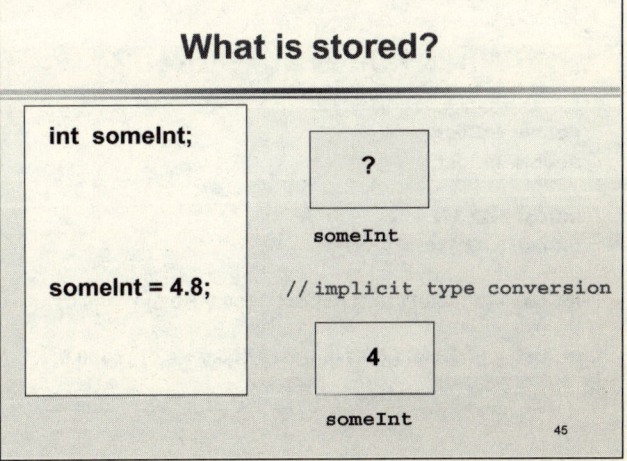

## What is stored?

```
int someInt;

someInt = 4.8;
```

// implicit type conversion

## Type Casting is Explicit Conversion of Type

```
int(4.8)                    has value  4

double(5)                   has value  5.0

double(7/4)                 has value  1.0

double(7) / double(4)       has value  1.75
```

## Some Expressions

int age;

| EXAMPLE | VALUE |
|---|---|
| 5 + 8 | 13 |
| 5 / 8 | 0 |
| 6.0 / 5.0 | 1.2 |
| double ( 4 / 8 ) | 0.0 |
| double ( 4 ) / 8 | 0.5 |

## What values are stored?

```
double  loCost;
double  hiCost;

loCost = 12.342;
hiCost = 12.348;

loCost = (double) ( (int) (loCost * 100.0 + 0.5) ) / 100.0;

hiCost = (double) ( (int) (hiCost * 100.0 + 0.5) ) / 100.0;
```

**Notes**

## Values were rounded to 2 decimal places

12.34
loCost

12.35
hiCost

## Method Call

- A method call temporarily transfers control to the called method's code to perform a task.

- When the method's code has finished executing, control is transferred back to the calling block.

## Where are Java methods?

located in packages

OR

written by programmers

### Write a Java expression . . .

To find the larger of myAge and yourAge and place it in variable older

```
int older;
```

52

### Write a Java expression . . .

To find the larger of myAge and yourAge and place it in variable older

```
int older;
. . .
older = Math.max ( myAge, yourAge );
```

53

### Write a Java expression . . .

To find the square root of $b^2 - 4ac$ and place it in variable d.

```
double a, b, c, d;
```

54

**Notes**

### Write a Java expression . . .

To find the square root of $b^2$ - 4ac and place it in variable d.

```
double a, b, c, d;
. . .
d = Math.sqrt ( b * b - 4.0 * a * c );
```

### Two Kinds of Methods

| Value-Returning | Void |
|---|---|
| Always is called as part of an expression. | Always is called as a separate statement. |
| Does some task. | Does some task. |
| Returns a value that takes its place in the expression. | Never returns a value to its caller. |

### Method Call Syntax

MethodName( Parameter List )

The parameter list is used to communicate values to the method by passing information.

The parameter list can contain 0, 1, or more parameters, separated by commas, depending on the method.

## `length` method

- Method `length` returns an `int` value that equals the number of characters in the string.

- You must use dot notation and parentheses in the call to method `length`.

## `indexOf` method

- Method `indexOf` searches a string to find a particular substring, and returns an `int` value that is the beginning position for the first occurrence of that substring within the string.

- The substring argument can be a literal `String`, a `String` expression, or a `char` value.

- If the substring could not be not found, method `indexOf` returns value `-1`.

## `substring` method

- Method `substring` returns a particular substring of a string, but does not change the string itself.

- The first parameter is an `int` that specifies a starting position within the string.

- The second parameter is an `int` that is 1 more than the ending position of the substring.

- Positions of characters within a string are numbered starting from 0, not from 1.

**Notes**

# Notes

## What value is returned?

// Using methods length, indexOf, substring

String stateName = "Mississippi" ;

stateName.length( )
stateName.indexOf("is")
stateName.substring( 0, 4 )
stateName.substring( 4, 6 )
stateName.substring( 9, 11 )

## What value is returned?

// Using methods length, indexOf, substring

String stateName = "Mississippi" ;

| | |
|---|---|
| stateName.length( ) | value 11 |
| stateName.indexOf("is") | value 1 |
| stateName.substring( 0, 4 ) | value "Miss" |
| stateName.substring( 4, 6 ) | value "is" |
| stateName.substring( 9, 11 ) | value "pi" |

## Map Measurement Case Study

- You want a program to determine walking distances between 4 sights in the city.
- Your city map legend says one inch on the map equals 1/4 mile in the city.
- You use the measured distances between 4 sights on the map.
- Display the walking distances (rounded to the nearest tenth) between each of the 4 sights.

## Java Case Study Program

```
// *******************************************************
// Walk program
// This program computes the mileage (rounded to nearest
// tenth of mile) for each of 4 distances, given the
// measurements on a map with scale of 1 in = 0.25 mile
// *******************************************************
import java.awt.*;             // Import Frame type
import java.awt.event.*;       // Import event handling
public class Walk
{
  private static Frame out;    // Declare Frame variable

  public static void main( String args[] )
  {

      final double SCALE = 0.25;              // Map scale
```

## Java Case Study Continued

```
      final double  DISTANCE1 = 1.5;  // First map measurement
      final double  DISTANCE2 = 2.3;  // Second map measurement
      final double  DISTANCE3 = 5.9;  // Third map measurement
      final double  DISTANCE4 = 4.0;  // Fourth map measurement

      double totMiles;                // Total of rounded miles
      double  miles;                  // One rounded mileage

      out = new Frame( );             // Instantiate Frame object
      out.setLayout( new GridLayout(0,1) );

      totMiles = 0.0;                 // Initialize total miles
```

```
      // Compute and round miles for first and second distances

      miles = (double)((int)(DISTANCE1 * SCALE * 10.0 + 0.5))
                      / 10.0;

      out.add( new Label ("Measurement of " + DISTANCE1
                          + " inches on map is "
                          + miles + " mile(s) long."));

      totMiles = totMiles + miles;

      miles = (double)((int)(DISTANCE2 * SCALE * 10.0 + 0.5))
                      / 10.0;

      out.add( new Label ("Measurement of " + DISTANCE2
                          + " inches on map is "
                          + miles + " mile(s) long."));

      totMiles = totMiles + miles;
```

**Notes**

```
// Compute and round miles for third and fourth distances

miles = (double)((int)(DISTANCE3 * SCALE * 10.0 + 0.5))
                / 10.0;

out.add( new Label ("Measurement of " + DISTANCE3
                        + " inches on map is "
                        + miles + " mile(s) long."));

totMiles = totMiles + miles;

miles = (double)((int)(DISTANCE4 * SCALE * 10.0 + 0.5))
                / 10.0;

out.add( new Label ("Measurement of " + DISTANCE4
                        + " inches on map is "
                        + miles + " mile(s) long."));

totMiles = totMiles + miles;
```

```
        out.add( new Label("Total mileage is "
                        + totMiles + " miles.") );
        out.pack( );              // Pack the frame
        out.show( );              // Show frame on screen
    // Event handler for window closing
        out.addWindowListener( new WindowAdapter( )
    // Create a WindowClosing method
            {
                public void windowClosing (WindowEvent event)
                {
                    out.dispose( );        // Remove frame
                    System.exit(0);        // Quit program
                }
            });
    }
}
```

## Some Math class methods

| | |
|---|---|
| **Math.abs ( x )**<br>// absolute value of x | Math.abs( -9.8 ) is 9.8 |
| **Math.sqrt( x )**<br>// square root of a non-negative x | Math.sqrt( 9.0 ) is 3.0 |
| **Math.log ( x )**<br>// natural (base e) logarithm of x | Math.log( 1.0 ) is 0 |
| **Math.max ( x, y )**<br>// larger value of x and y | Math.max( 2.5, 6.7 ) is 6.7 |
| **Math.pow ( x, y )**<br>// x raised to the power y | Math.pow( 9, 0.5 ) is 3.0 |

The Student Lecture Companion

## Method Calls

A method call uses the name of the method followed by ( ) enclosing a list of parameters.

```
outputDisplay = new Frame( );
System.out.println( "Done" );
older = Math.max( myAge, yourAge );
number = Math.sqrt( 456.34 );
outputDisplay.dispose( );
System.exit(0);
```

A method call temporarily transfers control to the called method to perform its task.

## Type Cast Operation

A cast operation is used to explicitly request a type conversion.

```
int     intVar;
double  doubleVar = 104.8 ;

intVar = ( int ) doubleVar ;     // cast operation
```

| 104.8 | 104 |
| doubleVar | intVar |

## Java Operator Precedence
### (highest to lowest)

| Operator | Associativity |
| --- | --- |
| . [ ]   ( args ) | Left to right |
| unary:  ++  --  +  - | Right to left |
| new   ( type ) | Right to left |
| *   /   % | Left to right |
| +   - | Left to right |
| = | Right to left |

# Notes

## In Java,

The size of a Unicode char value is 2 bytes.

**'A'**

exactly two bytes of memory space

**Sizes of other data type values are also specified.**

## ASCII and Unicode

- ASCII (pronounced ask-key) is an older **character set** used to represent characters internally as integers.
- ASCII is a subset of the newer Unicode character set.
- Using ASCII the character 'A' is internally stored as integer 65. In both sets, the successive alphabet letters are stored as successive integers. This enables character comparisons with 'A' less than 'B', etc.

### ASCII (Printable) Character Set

| Left Digit(s) \ Right Digit | 0 | 1 | 2 | 3 | 4 | 5 | 6 | 7 | 8 | 9 |
|---|---|---|---|---|---|---|---|---|---|---|
| 3  |   |   |   | ! | " | # | $ | % | & | ' |
| 4  | ( | ) | * | + | , | - | . | / | 0 | 1 |
| 5  | 2 | 3 | 4 | 5 | 6 | 7 | 8 | 9 | : | ; |
| 6  | < | = | > | ? | @ | A | B | C | D | E |
| 7  | F | G | H | I | J | K | L | M | N | O |
| 8  | P | Q | R | S | T | U | V | W | X | Y |
| 9  | Z | [ | \ | ] | ^ | _ | ` | a | b | c |
| 10 | d | e | f | g | h | i | j | k | l | m |
| 11 | n | o | p | q | r | s | t | u | v | w |
| 12 | x | y | z | { | | | } | ~ |   |   |   |

## Implicit type conversion occurs . . .

**Whenever values of different data types are used in:**

1. arithmetic expressions
2. assignment operations

### TWO RULES APPLY . . .

---

## A widening conversion . . .

- **Is a type conversion that does not result in a loss of information. Specifically, for mixed type expressions using both integer and floating-point type values:**

    Step 1. The integer value is temporarily converted to a floating-point value.

    Step 2. The operation is performed.

    Step 3. The result is a floating-point value.

---

## A narrowing conversion . . .

- **Is a type conversion that** may result in a loss of information.

**FOR EXAMPLE,**  98.6   98
                temperature  number

```
double  temperature = 98.6 ;
int  number ;
number = temperature ;     // loss occurs
```

# Chapter 5: Event-Driven Input and Software Design Strategies

**Notes**

### Introduction to Java and Software Design

Dale • Weems • Headington

**Chapter 5**
Event-Driven Input and Software Design Strategies

### Chapter 5 Topics

- Declaring and Instantiating a `TextField`
- Declaring and Instantiating a `Button`
- Handling `Button` events with `actionPerformed`
- Converting strings into numeric types
- Using the object-oriented design (OOD) strategy
- Using CRC cards
- Using the Functional Decomposition strategy
- Using Pseudocode

### More of the `java.awt` Hierarchy

Object
├── Component
│   └── Container
│       └── Window
│           └── Frame
├── FlowLayout
├── BorderLayout
└── GridLayout

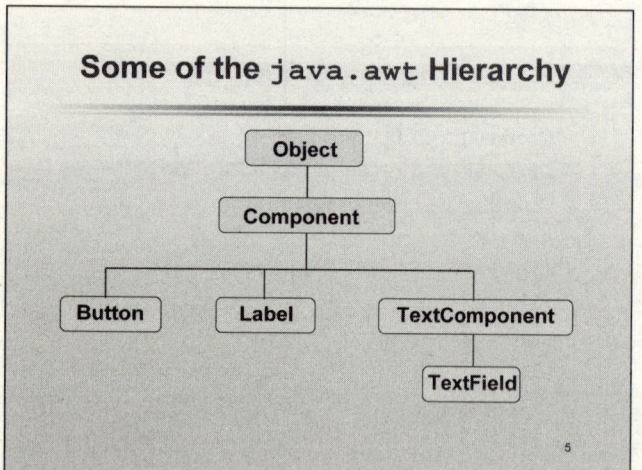

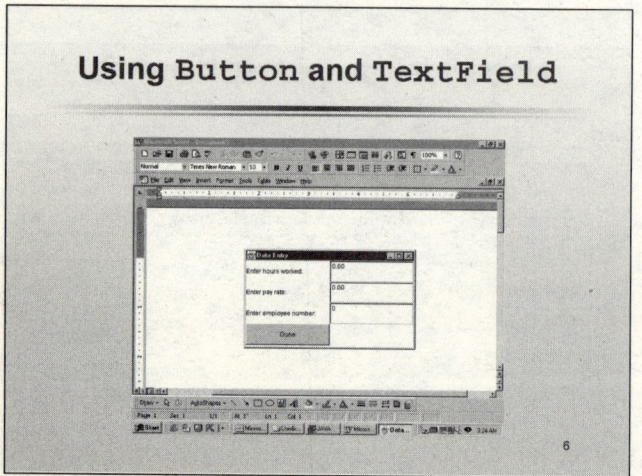

**Notes**

## Notes

### class TextField constructors

```
// Constructors
public TextField( int columns )
// Constructs a TextField with specified number of columns
public TextField( String s, int columns )
// Constructs a TextField with text s in specified number
// of columns
```

### class TextField methods

```
// Methods
public String getText( )
// Returns the TextField text
public void setText( String s )
// Sets the TextField text to the specified String
```

### class TextField

- TextField
- setText
- ⋮
- getText

Private data and methods

## Steps for using a Button

1. Declare a Button variable
2. Use new to instantiate the Button object
3. Give a name to the button event
4. Add the Button object to the container
5. Create and instantiate a listener class with actionPerformed to handle button events
6. Register the listener with the button by calling method addActionListener

## Using a Button

```
. . .
Frame inputFrame;

Button done;                          // Declare Button variable
ButtonHandler myHandler;
. . .
done = new Button("Done");            // Instantiate Button
done.setActionCommand("done");        // Name the button event
inputFrame.add(done);                 // Add the button to Frame

myHandler = new ButtonHandler( );     // Instantiate listener
done.addActionListener(myHandler);    // Register listener
. . .
```

## Handling an action event

- Button objects generate "action events" that can be processed by any ActionListener object.
- Any class that implements interface ActionListener must provide a definition of method actionPerformed.
- Once an ActionListener object is registered to "handle" an action event, method actionPerformed is called automatically whenever an action event occurs.

**Notes**

## Two of the event-listener interfaces in package `java.awt.event`

```
        java.util.EventListener
           /            \
   WindowListener    ActionListener
```

## Graphical User Interfaces

- GUIs are built from GUI components.
- GUI component classes are part of java.awt (Abstract Windowing Toolkit package).
- GUIs are event driven. They generate events when the user interacts with the GUI.
- An event is an action such as clicking the mouse, clicking a button, that takes place asynchronously (not at a particular time) with respect to the execution of the program.

## Delegation event model

- **Means** using event listeners for event handling.
- **The handling** of an event is delegated to a particular object in the program.
- **Using** a separate class to define an event listener is a common practice for separating the GUI interface from the implementation of its event handler.

## 2 Steps for processing an event

- **Register an event listener** object to "listen" for specific types of events.
- **Implement event handler method(s)** to be called automatically in response to a particular type of event.
- **A class that implements an event listener interface must provide a definition for every method of that interface.**

## Syntax for Instance Method Call

**InstanceMethodCall**

> ObjectName.MethodName ( parameter , parameter . . . );

**EXAMPLES**

```
outDisplay.show( );
System.out.println("Good morning.");
outputDisplay.add( new Label("Total") );
```

## Syntax for Class Method Call

**ClassMethodCall**

> ClassName.ClassMethodName ( parameter , parameter . . . );

**EXAMPLES**

```
double number;
Double someDouble;
number = Math.sqrt(456.34);
someDouble = Double.valueOf("55.43");
```

## Notes

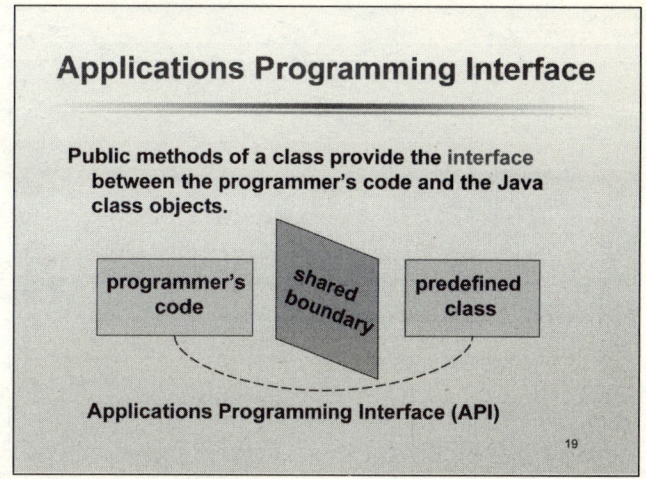

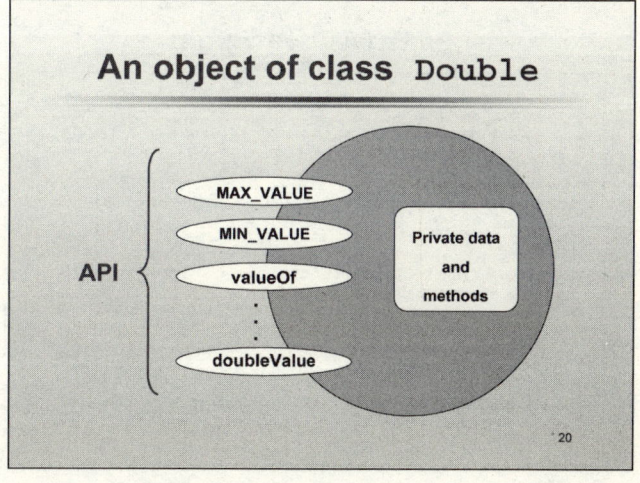

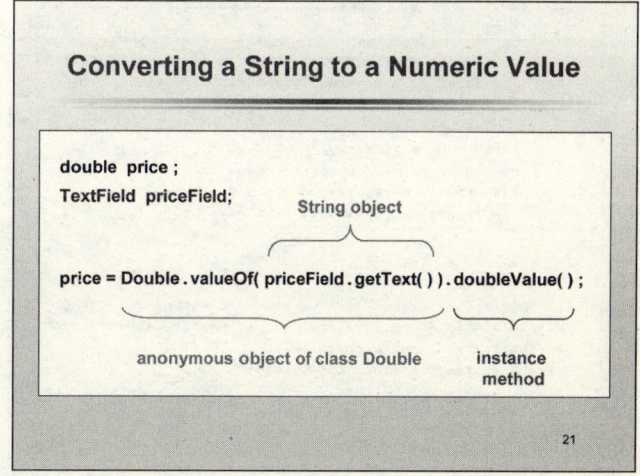

## Cascading Method Calls

```
int quantity ;
TextField quantityField;
                            String object
                         ⎧―――――――――――⎫
quantity = Integer.valueOf( quantityField.getText( ) ).intValue( );
           ⎩―――――――――――――――――――――――――⎭  ⎩――――⎭
           anonymous object of class Integer      instance
                                                  method
```

22

## Rainfall Program

```
// ********************************************************
// Rainfall program
// Prints a running average of rainfall amounts.
// ********************************************************
import  java.awt.*;            // User interface classes
import  java.awt.event.*;      // Event handling classes

public class Rainfall
{
  // Define a button listener
  private static class ActionHandler
                              implements ActionListener
  {
    public void actionPerformed(ActionEvent event)
    // Handles events from the Enter button in inputFrame
    {
      double amount;            // Holds an input value
      double average;           // Holds computed average
```

23

```
      // Convert string from inputField to a double value
      amount =  Double.valueOf(inputField.getText())
                                       .doubleValue();
      numberEntries++;
      total = total + amount;
      average = total / numberEntries;
      outputLabel.setText("" + average);
      inputField.setText("");        // Clear input field
    }
  }

  // Declare class variables for class Rainfall
  private static Frame inputFrame;    // User interface frame
  private static Label outputLabel;
  private static TextField inputField;
  private static double total;        // Keeps running total
  private static double numberEntries; // Counts entries
```

24

# Notes

```java
public static void main( String[ ] args )
{
    Label entryLabel;              // Label for input field
    Button enter;                  // Enter button
    ActionHandler action;          // Declare listener

    // Initialize and instantiate variables
    total = 0.0;
    numberEntries = 0.0;
    inputFrame = new Frame( );
    entryLabel = new Label("Enter amount here:");
    outputLabel = new Label("0.0", Label.RIGHT);
    inputField = new TextField("", 10);
    enter = new Button("Enter");
    enter.setActionCommand("enter"); // Name button event
    action = new ActionHandler( );   // Instantiate listener
    enter.addActionListener(action); // Register listener
```

```java
    // Add components to frame
    inputFrame.setLayout(new GridLayout(2,2));
    inputFrame.add(entryLabel);
    inputFrame.add(inputField);        // Add textfield
    inputFrame.add(enter);             // Add button
    inputFrame.add(outputLabel);
    inputFrame.pack( );
    inputFrame.show( );

    inputFrame.addWindowListener( new WindowAdapter( )
    // Declare window closing event handler
        {
            public void windowClosing (WindowEvent event)
            {
                inputFrame.dispose( );    // Remove frame
                System.exit( 0 );         // Quit program
            }
        });
}
```

## Software Design Strategies

**FUNCTIONAL DECOMPOSITION**

The problem is divided into **more easily handled subproblems**, the solutions of which together create a solution to the overall problem.

**OBJECT-ORIENTED DESIGN**

The solution is expressed in terms of **objects** (self-contained entities composed of data and operations on that data) that interact by sending messages to one another.

## What is an object?

set of methods
(public member functions)

**OBJECT**

Private data and methods

internal state
(values of private data members)

## Inheritance

- Enables us to define a new class by adapting the definition of an existing class to satisfy additional responsibilities.

- Inheritance of properties is one characteristic of an object-oriented programming language.

## Superclass and Subclass

- Inheritance enables us to define a new class (called a subclass) that inherits the properties (both data fields and methods) of an already existing class.

- The newly derived class is then specialized by adding properties specific to it.

- The class being inherited from is the superclass.

- The class that inherits properties is the subclass.

**Notes**

**Notes**

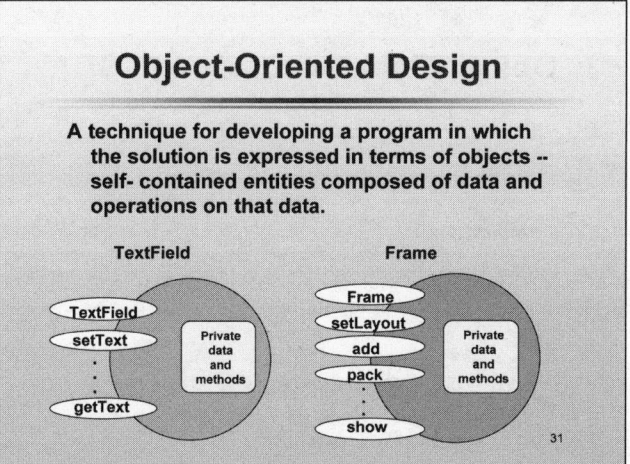

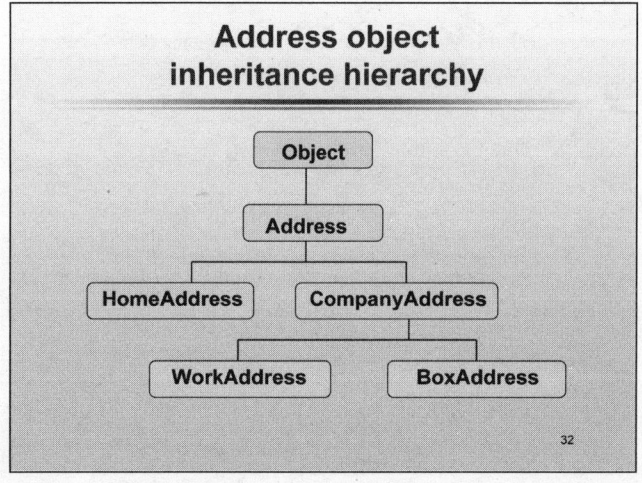

## Object-Oriented Design (OOD)

**FOCUS** is on the entities (objects) in a problem.

**BEGINS** by identifying the classes of objects in the problem, and choosing appropriate operations on those objects.

**PROGRAMS** are collections of objects that communicate with (send messsages to) each other.

**DATA** plays a leading role. Algorithms are used to implement operations on the objects and to enable interaction of objects with each other.

## Why use OOD with large software projects?

- Objects within a program often model real-life objects in the problem to be solved.

- The OOD concept of inheritance allows the customization of an existing class to meet particular needs. This can reduce the time and effort needed to design, implement, and maintain large systems.

## Functional Decomposition

A technique for developing a program in which the problem is divided into more easily handled subproblems, the solutions of which create a solution to the overall problem.

In functional decomposition, we work from the abstract (a list of the major solution steps for which some implementation details remain unspecified) to the concrete (algorithmic steps for which the implementation details are fully specified).

**Notes**

**Notes**

## Functional Decomposition

FOCUS is on the sequence of actions (algorithms) required to solve the problem.

BEGINS by breaking the solution into a series of major steps. This process continues until each subproblem cannot be divided further or has an obvious solution.

PROGRAMS are collections of modules that solve subproblems. A module structure chart (hierarchical solution tree) is often created.

DATA plays a secondary role in support of actions.

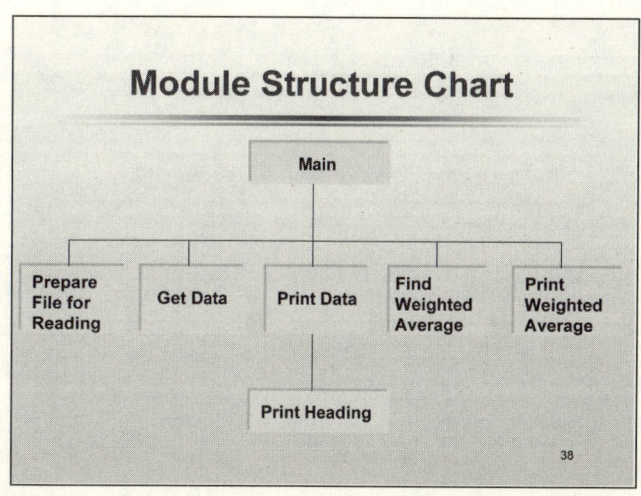

## Module Structure Chart

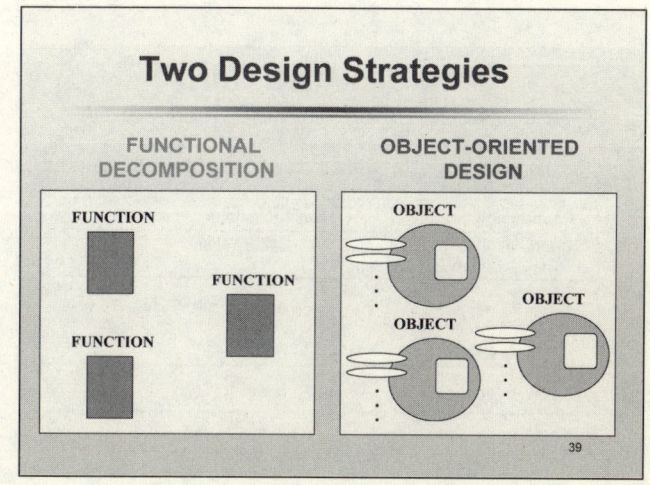

## Two Design Strategies

## CRC Cards

- The use of Classes, Responsibilities and Collaborations (CRC) cards is an informal technique for developing objected-oriented designs.
- For each class, a CRC card is created listing the class responsibilities and collaborations.
- Brainstorming, walk-throughs and scenarios are used to identify and refine the classes needed for the problem.

## Blank CRC Card

| Class Name: | Superclass: | Subclasses: |
|---|---|---|
| Responsibilities | Collaborations | |
| | | |
| | | |
| | | |
| | | |

## Address CRC Card

| Class Name: Address | Superclass: Object | Subclasses: HomeAddress, CompanyAddress |
|---|---|---|
| Responsibilities | Collaborations | |
| Create itself (name, city, state, zip code) | Name: Name | |
| Know its name | Name: First, Middle, Last | |
| Know its city | None | |
| Know its state | None | |
| Know its zip code | None | |

# Chapter 6: Conditions, Logical Expressions, and Selection Control Structures

**Notes**

---

### Introduction to
### Java and Software Design

Dale • Weems • Headington

Chapter 6

Conditions, Logical Expressions, and Selection Control Structures

---

### Chapter 6 Topics

- Java Control Structures
- `boolean` Data Type
- Using Relational and Logical Operators in Logical Expressions
- `if-else` Selection Structure
- `if` Selection Structure
- Nested `if` Statements
- Handling Multiple Button Events

---

### Flow of Control

- means the order in which the computer executes statements in a program.

WHAT ARE THE POSSIBILITIES...

## Flow of Control

**There are 5 general types of Java control structures:**

- Sequence (by default)
- Selection (also called branch or decision)
- Loop (also called repetition or iteration)
- Subprogram
- Asynchronous

## Java's 5 Basic Control Structures

- A **sequence** is a series of statements that executes one after another.
- **Selection** executes different statements depending on certain conditions.
- **Loop** repeats statements while certain conditions are met.
- A **subprogram** breaks the program into smaller units.
- **Asynchronous control** handles events that originate outside your program, such as button clicks.

## SEQUENCE

→ Statement → Statement → Statement → . . .

# Notes

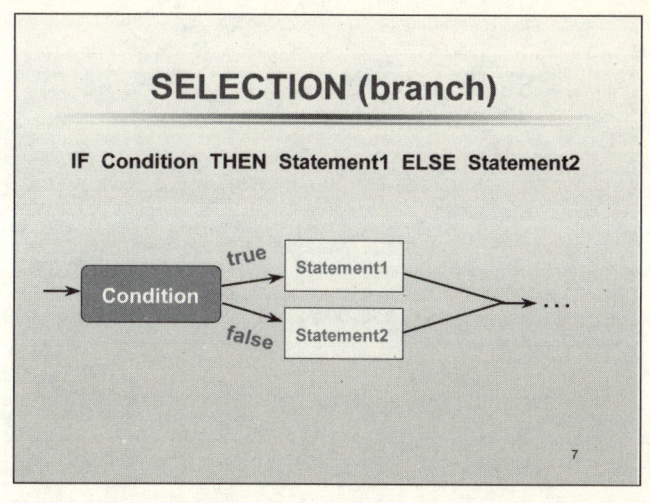

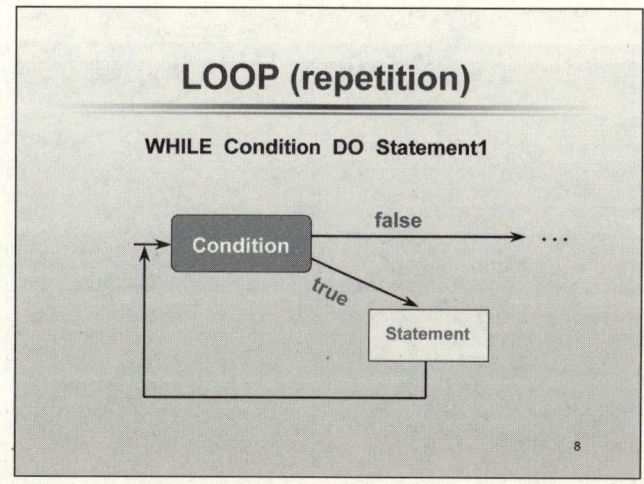

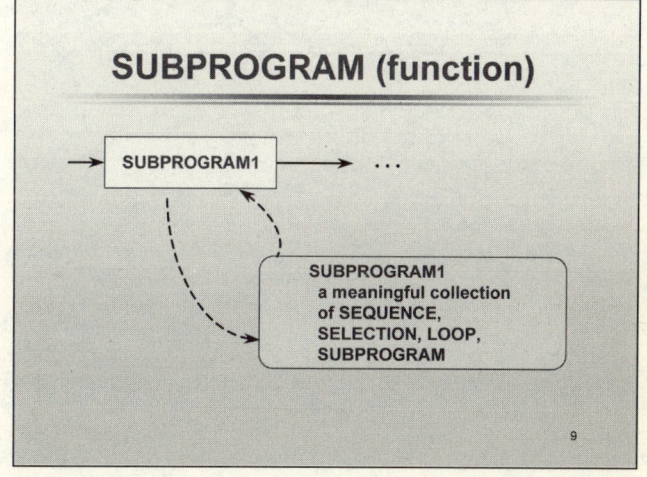

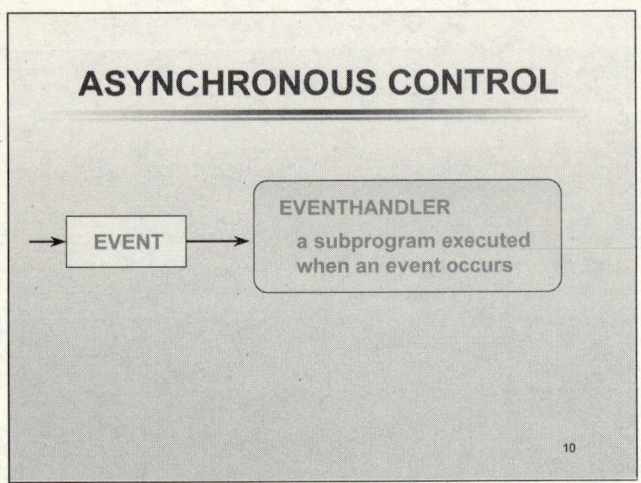

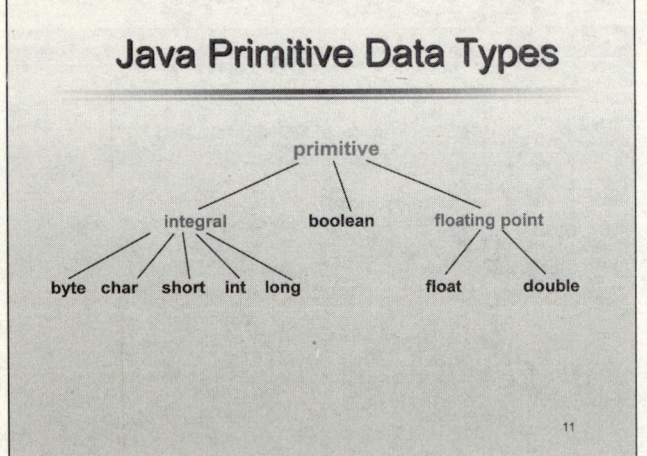

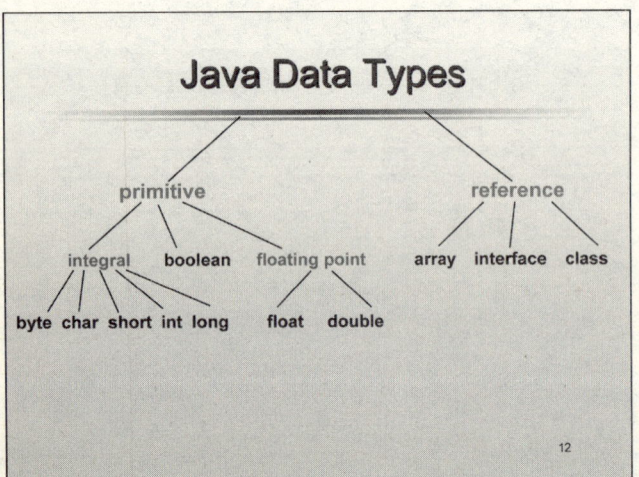

**Notes**

## Notes

### `boolean` Data Type

- Type `boolean` is a primitive type consisting of just 2 values, the constants true and false.
- We can declare variables of type boolean.

```
boolean   hasFever;    // true if has high temperature
boolean   isSenior;    // true if age is at least 55
```

### Expressions in Java

- "Boolean expression" means an expression whose value is true or false
- An expression is any valid combination of operators and operands
- Each expression has a value
- Use of parentheses is encouraged
- Otherwise, use precedence chart to determine order

| Primitive Data Type | Size (bits) | Values |
|---|---|---|
| boolean | 1 | true or false |
| char | 16 | '\u0000' to '\uFFFF' |
| byte | 8 | -128 to +127 |
| short | 16 | -32,768 to +32,767 |
| int | 32 | -2,147,483,648 to +2,147,483,647 |
| long | 64 | -9,233,372,036,854,775,808 to +9,233,372,036,854,775,807 |
| float | 32 | ±1.4E-45 to ±3.4028235E+38 |
| double | 64 | ±4.9E-324 to +1.7976931348623157E+308 |

## 6 Relational Operators

Are used in expressions of form:

| ExpressionA | Operator | ExpressionB |
|---|---|---|
| temperature | > | humidity |
| B * B - 4.0 * A * C | > | 0.0 |
| number | == | 35 |
| initial | != | 'Q' |

---

```
int x, y ;
x = 4;
y = 6;
```

| EXPRESSION | VALUE |
|---|---|
| x < y | true |
| x + 2 < y | false |
| x != y | true |
| x + 3 >= y | true |
| y == x | false |
| y == x+2 | true |

---

## Precedence

- **Higher Precedence** determines which operator is applied first in an expression having several operators.

# Notes

## Java Operator Precedence
### (highest to lowest)

| Operator | Associativity |
|---|---|
| . [ ]   ( args ) | Left to right |
| unary:  ++   --   +   - | Right to left |
| new   ( type ) | Right to left |
| *   /   % | Left to right |
| +   - | Left to right |
| = | Right to left |

## Some Java Operators

| Precedence | Operator | Description |
|---|---|---|
| Higher | ( ) | Parentheses |
|  | + | Positive |
|  | - | Negative |
|  | * | Multiplication |
|  | / | Division |
|  | % | Modulus (remainder) |
|  | + | Addition |
|  | - | Subtraction |
| Lower | = | Assignment |

## In Java,

The size of a Unicode char value is 2 bytes.

**'A'**

exactly two bytes of memory space

**Sizes of other data type values are also specified.**

## ASCII and Unicode

- **ASCII (pronounced ask-key) is an older character set** used to represent characters internally as integers.
- **ASCII is a subset of the newer Unicode character set.**
- **Using ASCII the character 'A' is internally stored as integer 65.** In both sets, the successive alphabet letters are stored as successive integers. This enables character comparisons with 'A' less than 'B', etc.

### ASCII (Printable) Character Set

| Left Digit(s) \ Right Digit | 0 | 1 | 2 | 3 | 4 | 5 | 6 | 7 | 8 | 9 |
|---|---|---|---|---|---|---|---|---|---|---|
| 3 |   |   | ☺ | ! | " | # | $ | % | & | ' |
| 4 | ( | ) | * | + | , | - | . | / | 0 | 1 |
| 5 | 2 | 3 | 4 | 5 | 6 | 7 | 8 | 9 | : | ; |
| 6 | < | = | > | ? | @ | A | B | C | D | E |
| 7 | F | G | H | I | J | K | L | M | N | O |
| 8 | P | Q | R | S | T | U | V | W | X | Y |
| 9 | Z | [ | \ | ] | ^ | _ | ` | a | b | c |
| 10 | d | e | f | g | h | i | j | k | l | m |
| 11 | n | o | p | q | r | s | t | u | v | w |
| 12 | x | y | z | { | | | } | ~ |   |   |   |

## Comparing Strings

| Method Name | Parameter Type | Returns | Operation Performed |
|---|---|---|---|
| equals | String | boolean | Tests for equality of string contents. |
| compareTo | String | int | Returns 0 if equal, a positive integer if the string in the parameter comes before the string associated with the method and a negative integer if the parameter comes after it. |

**Notes**

```
String   myState;
String   yourState;
myState = "Texas";
yourState = "Maryland";
```

| EXPRESSION | VALUE |
|---|---|
| myState.equals(yourState) | false |
| 0 < myState.compareTo(yourState) | true |
| myState.equals("Texas") | true |
| 0 > myState.compareTo("texas") | true |

## Comparing Strings

| Method Name | Parameter Type | Returns | Operation Performed |
|---|---|---|---|
| toLowerCase | none | String | Returns a new identical string, except the characters are all lowercase. |
| toUpperCase | none | String | Returns a new identical string, except the characters are all uppercase. |

## Java control statements

- **Selection**
    - if
    - if - else
    - switch
- **Repetition**
    - while
    - for
    - do - while

## Control Structures

**Use logical expressions which may include:**

*6 Relational Operators*

    <    <=    >    >=    ==    !=

| Operator | Meaning | Associativity |
|---|---|---|
| ! | NOT | Right |
| *, / , % | Multiplication, Division, Modulus | Left |
| + , - | Addition, Subtraction | Left |
| < | Less than | Left |
| <= | Less than or equal to | Left |
| > | Greater than | Left |
| >= | Greater than or equal to | Left |
| == | Is equal to | Left |
| != | Is not equal to | Left |
| && | AND | Left |
| \|\| | OR | Left |
| = | Assignment | Right |

## Control Structures

**Use logical expressions which may include:**

*6 Relational Operators*

    <    <=    >    >=    ==    !=

*6 Logical Operators*

    !    &&    \|\|    ^    &    \|

# Notes

| LOGICAL EXPRESSION | MEANING | DESCRIPTION |
|---|---|---|
| ! p | NOT p | ! p is false if p is true<br>! p is true if p is false |
| p && q | p AND q | p && q is true if both p and q are true. It is false otherwise. |
| p \|\| q | p OR q | p \|\| q is true if either p or q or both are true. It is false otherwise. |

## What is the value of each expression?

```
  100       -13        27
 grade    number      hour
```

( grade >= 60 )

( number > 0 )

( hour >= 0 && hour < 24 )

( hour == 12 \|\| hour == 0 )

```
int    age ;
boolean  isSenior, hasFever ;
double  temperature ;
age = 20;
temperature = 102.0 ;
isSenior = (age >= 55) ;           // isSenior is false
hasFever = (temperature > 98.6) ;  // hasFever is true
```

| EXPRESSION | VALUE |
|---|---|
| isSenior && hasFever | false |
| isSenior \|\| hasFever | true |
| ! isSenior | true |
| ! hasFever | false |

## What is the value?

```
int  age, height;
age = 25;
height = 70;
```

| EXPRESSION | VALUE |
|---|---|
| !(age < 10) | ? |
| !(height > 60) | ? |

## "Short-Circuit" Evaluation

- Java uses short circuit evaluation of logical expressions with operators ! && ||

- this means logical expressions are evaluated left to right and evaluation stops as soon as the final truth value can be determined

## Short-Circuit Example

```
int  age, height;
age = 25;
height = 70;
```

EXPRESSION

(age > 50)  &&  (height > 60)

false

Evaluation can stop now because result of && is only true when both sides are true. It is already determined that the entire expression will be false.

# Notes

## More Short-Circuiting

```
int   age, height;
age = 25;
height = 70;
```

**EXPRESSION**

(height > 60)  ||  (age > 40)

true

Evaluation can stop now because result of || is true if one side is true. It is already determined that the entire expression will be true.

## What happens?

```
int   age, weight;
age = 25;
weight = 145;
```

**EXPRESSION**

(weight < 180)  &&  (age >= 20)

true

Must still be evaluated because truth value of entire expression is not yet known. Why? Result of && is only true if both sides are true.

## What happens?

```
int   age, height;
age = 25;
height = 70;
```

**EXPRESSION**

! (height > 60)  ||  (age > 50)

true

false

Does this part need to be evaluated?

### Write an expression for each

taxRate is over 25% and income is less than $20000

temperature is less than or equal to 75 or humidity is less than 70%

age is over 21 and age is less than 60

age is 21 or 22

### Some Answers

(taxRate > .25)  &&  (income < 20000)

(temperature <= 75)  ||  (humidity < .70)

(age > 21)  &&  (age < 60)

(age == 21)  ||  (age == 22)

### Use Precedence Chart

```
int    number ;
double  x ;
       number != 0  &&  x < 1 / number
```

| / | has highest priority |
| < | next priority |
| != | next priority |
| && | next priority |

What happens if number has value 0?
   Run Time Error (Division by zero) occurs.

**Notes**

## Short-Circuit Benefits

- One Boolean expression can be placed first to "guard" a potentially unsafe operation in a second Boolean expression

- Time is saved in evaluation of complex expressions using operators || and &&

## Our Example Revisited

```
int    number;
double x;

( number != 0) && ( x < 1 / number )
```
is evaluated first and has value false

Because operator is &&, the entire expression will have value false. Due to short-circuiting the right side is not evaluated in Java.

## What can go wrong here?

```
int   average;
int   total;
int   counter;
   .
   .
   .
average = total / counter ;
```

## Improved Version

```
double  average,
int   total;
int   counter;

...        // processing total

if ( counter != 0 )
{
        average = (double) total / counter ;    // cast operator
        System.out.println( "Average is " + average );
}
else
        System.out.println( "None were entered" );
```

## `if-else` Syntax

> **if** ( *Expression* )
>     **Statement1A**
> **else**
>     **Statement1B**

NOTE: Statement1A and Statement1B each can be a single statement, a null statement, or a block.

## `if-else` selection control structure

**Provides two-way selection**

```
         expression
       true  /  \  false
            /    \
    statement1A  statement1B
```

## Notes

### Style when using blocks

```
if ( Expression )
{
                    ⎫
                    ⎬  "if branch"
}                   ⎭
else
{
                    ⎫
                    ⎬  "else branch"
}                   ⎭
```

---

```
int    carDoors, driverAge ;
float  premium, monthlyPayment ;
. . .
if ( (carDoors == 4 ) && (driverAge > 24) )
{      premium = 650.00 ;
       System.out.println( "Low Risk" );
}
else
{      premium = 1200.00 ;
       System.out.println( "High Risk" );
}

monthlyPayment = premium / 12.0 + 5.00 ;
```

---

### What happens if you omit braces?

```
if ( (carDoors == 4 ) && (driverAge > 24) )
      premium = 650.00 ;
      System.out.println( "Low Risk" );
else
      premium = 1200.00 ;
      System.out.println( "High Risk" );

monthlyPayment = premium / 12.0 + 5.00 ;
```

**COMPILE ERROR OCCURS.** The "if branch" is the single statement following the if.

## `if-else` for a mail order

Assign value .25 to `discountRate` and assign value 10.00 to `shipCost` if `purchase` is over 100.00

Otherwise, assign value .15 to `discountRate` and assign value 5.00 to `shipCost`

Either way, calculate `totalBill`

## These braces cannot be omitted

```
if ( purchase > 100.00 )
{
      discountRate = .25 ;
      shipCost  = 10.00 ;
}
else
{
      discountRate = .15 ;
      shipCost  = 5.00 ;
}

totalBill = purchase * (1.0 - discountRate) + shipCost ;
```

## Braces can only be omitted when each branch is a single statement

```
if ( lastInitial  <= 'K' )
        volume = 1;
else
        volume = 2;

System.out.println( "Look it up in volume # "
          + volume + " of NYC phone book" );
```

## Notes

### `if` statement is a selection

of whether or not to execute a statement

### `if` Syntax

```
if ( Expression )
    statement
```

NOTE: statement can be a single statement, a null statement, or a block.

### Write `if` statement two ways

If taxCode has value 'T', increase price by adding taxRate times price to it.

## One Answer

```
if ( taxCode == 'T' )
    price = price + taxRate * price;
```

## The statements in an `if` form

can be any kind of statement, including another selection structure or repetition structure.

## Multiway selection

is also called multiway branching, and

can be accomplished by using NESTED if statements.

**Notes**

## Nested if statements

```
if ( Expression1 )
       Statement1
else if ( Expression2 )
       Statement2
            .
            .
            .
else if ( ExpressionN )
       StatementN
else
       Statement N+1
```
EXACTLY 1 of these statements will be executed.

## Nested if statements

Each Expression is evaluated in sequence, until some Expression is found that is true.

Only the specific Statement following that particular true Expression is executed.

If no Expression is true, the Statement following the final else is executed.

Actually, the final else and final Statement are optional. If omitted, and no Expression is true, then no Statement is executed.

AN EXAMPLE . . .

## Multiway branching

```
if ( creditsEarned >= 90 )
       System.out.println( "Senior Status" );
else if ( creditsEarned >= 60 )
       System.out.println( "Junior Status" );
else if ( creditsEarned >= 30 )
       System.out.println( "Sophomore Status" );
else
       System.out.println( "Freshman Status" );
```

## Writing Nested if statements

Display one word to describe
the int value of number
as "Positive", "Negative", or "Zero"

## One answer

```
if (number > 0)
      System.out.println( "Positive" );
else if (number < 0)
      System.out.println( "Positive" );
else
      System.out.println( "Zero" );
```

## In the absence of braces,

an else is always paired with the
closest preceding `if` that doesn't
already have an `else` paired with it.

## Notes

### Bad Example has output: FAIL

```
double average;
average = 100.0;
if ( average >= 60.0 )
    if ( average < 70.0 )
        System.out.println( "Marginal PASS" );
else
    System.out.println( "FAIL" );
```

100.0
average

WHY?  The compiler ignores indentation
      and pairs the else with the second if.

### To correct the problem, use braces

```
double average;
average = 100.0;
if ( average >= 60.0 )
{
    if ( average < 70.0 )
        System.out.println( "Marginal PASS" );
}
else
    System.out.println( "FAIL" );
```

100.0
average

### Floating-point values

- Do not compare floating-point values for equality.
- Instead, compare them for near-equality.

```
double  myNumber;
double  yourNumber;
 . . .
if  ( Math.abs (myNumber - yourNumber) < 0.00001 )
    System.out.println( "Close enough!" );
```

## Some of the `java.awt` Hierarchy

Object → Component → Button, Label, TextComponent → TextField

## Processing an action event

- `Button` objects generate "action events" that can be processed by any ActionListener object.

- Any class that implements interface ActionListener must provide a definition of method actionPerformed.

- Once an ActionListener object is registered to "handle" a button's action event, its method actionPerformed is called automatically whenever that button's action event occurs.

## Delegation event model

- Means the use of event listeners in event handling. The handling of an event is delegated to a particular object in the program.

- When there are several buttons in the program, they can all have the same event handler, or they can have different event handlers.

- If several buttons have the same event handler, you can use selection in method actionPerformed to determine which button fired an event.

Notes

# Notes

## Calculator CRC Card

| Class Name: Calculator | Superclass: | Subclasses: |
|---|---|---|
| **Responsibilities** | **Collaborations** ||
| Prepare window for input | Textfield, Label, String, Buttons ||
| Handle numeric button events | Buttons, register (text field) ||
| Handle clear button event | Button, register (text field) ||
| Handle window closing | Frame ||

## Calculator Program

```java
// ************************************************
// Calculator program
// Simulates a simple calculator.
// ************************************************
import java.awt.*;         // User interface classes
import java.awt.event.*;   // Event handling classes

public class Calculator
{
  // Define action listener for numeric buttons
  private static class NumericHandler
                        implements ActionListener
  {
    public void actionPerformed(ActionEvent event)
    // Handles events from numeric buttons in calcFrame
    {
      double secondOperand;   // Holds an input value
      String whichButton;     // Holds button's name
```

```java
// Calculator Program Part 2

      // Get the operand
      secondOperand = Double.valueOf(inputField.getText())
                                     .doubleValue();

      whichButton = event.getActionCommand( ); // Get name

      if (whichButton.equals("add"))
         result = result + SecondOperand;
      else
         result = result - SecondOperand;

      register.setText("" + result);   // Display result
      inputField.setText("");          // Clear input
    }
  }
```

The Student Lecture Companion

```
// Calculator Program Part 3

    // Define action listener for Clear button
    private static class ClearHandler
                            implements ActionListener
    {
        public void actionPerformed(ActionEvent event)
        // Handles events from Clear button in calcFrame
        {
            result = 0.0;                // Set back to zero
            register.setText("0.0");     // Reset register
            inputField.setText("");      // Clear input
        }
    }

    // Declare class variables for class Calculator

    private static Frame calcFrame;      // Interface frame
    private static Label register;       // Result shown on screen
    private static TextField inputField;
    private static double result;        // Keeps current value
```

```
// Calculator Program Part 4

    public static void main( String[ ] args )
    {
        Label resultLabel;         // Indicates output area
        Label entryLabel;          // Label for input field
        Button add;                // Add button
        Button subtract;           // Subtract button
        Button clear;              // Clear  button
        NumericHandler operation;  // Declare numeric listener
        clearHandler clear operation; // Declare clear listener

        // Instantiate event handlers

        operation = new NumericHandler( );
        clearOperation = new ClearHandler( );
        result = 0.0;
```

```
// Calculator Program Part 5

    // Instantiate labels and initialize input field

    calcFrame = new Frame( );
    calcFrame.setLayout(new GridLayout(4, 2));
    resultLabel = new Label("Result:");
    register = new Label("0.0", Label.RIGHT);
    entryLabel = new Label("Enter #:");
    inputField = new TextField("", 10);

    // Instantiate button objects
    add = new Button("+");
    subtract = new Button("-");
    clear = new Button("Clear");

    // Name button events
    add.setActionCommand("add");
    subtract.setActionCommand("subtract");
    clear.setActionCommand("clear");
```

# Notes

```
// Calculator Program Part 6

    // Register the button listeners
    add.addActionListener(operation);
    subtract.addActionListener(operation);
    clear.addActionListener(clearOperation);

    // Add components to calcFrame
    calcFrame.add(resultLabel);
    calcFrame.add(register);
    calcFrame.add(entryLabel);
    calcFrame.add(inputField);
    calcFrame.add(add);
    calcFrame.add(subtract);
    calcFrame.add(clear);
    calcFrame.pack( );
    calcFrame.show( );
    calcFrame.addWindowListener( new WindowAdapter( )
```

## End of Calculator Program

```
    calcFrame.addWindowListener( new WindowAdapter( )
    // Declare window closing event handler
      {
         public void windowClosing (WindowEvent event)
         {
            calcFrame.dispose( );    // Remove frame
            System.exit( 0 );        // Quit program
         }
      });
  }
}
```

# Chapter 7: Classes and Methods

## Introduction to Java and Software Design

Dale • Weems • Headington

Chapter 7

Classes and Methods

## Chapter 7 Topics

- Abstraction and encapsulation in OOD
- Designing the public interface for a class
- Designing a class constructor
- Data lifetime
- Declaring methods
- Parameter passing
- Collecting classes in a package

## Java Data Types

- primitive
  - integral: byte, char, short, int, long
  - boolean
  - floating point: float, double
- reference
  - array
  - interface
  - class

**Notes**

## Encapsulation

Class implementation details are hidden from the programmer who uses the class. This is called encapsulation.

Public methods of a class provide the interface between the application code and the class objects.

| programmer's application code | abstraction barrier | class implementation details |

## Benefits of encapsulation

- **Protects** class contents from being damaged by external code.
- **Simplifies** the design of large programs by developing parts in isolation from each other.
- Allows **modifiability** of the class implementation after its initial development.
- Allows **reuse** of a class in other applications, and extension of the class to form new related classes.

## Encapsulated vs. Exposed Implementation

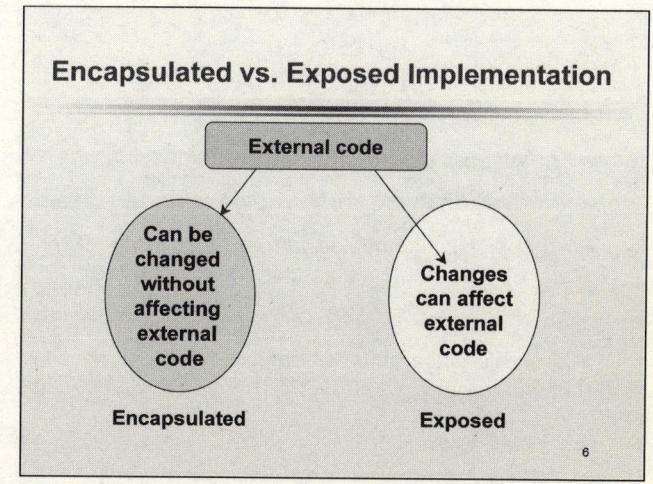

## Reuse of Vehicle Class

Vehicle Class
- Vehicle Use Scheduling Program
- Vehicle Maintenance Scheduling Program
- Vehicle Tax Accounting Program

## Abstraction

**Data abstraction** is the separation of the logical representation of an object's range of values from their implementation.

**Control abstraction** is the separation of the logical properties of the operations on an object from their implementation.

class logical representation and properties → abstraction barrier → class implementation details

## Object State

- The object's state is the current set of values that it contains.

- An object is instantiated with an initial state. If any of its methods can subsequently change its state, the object is said to be mutable.

- Methods that change an object's state are called transformers.

# Notes

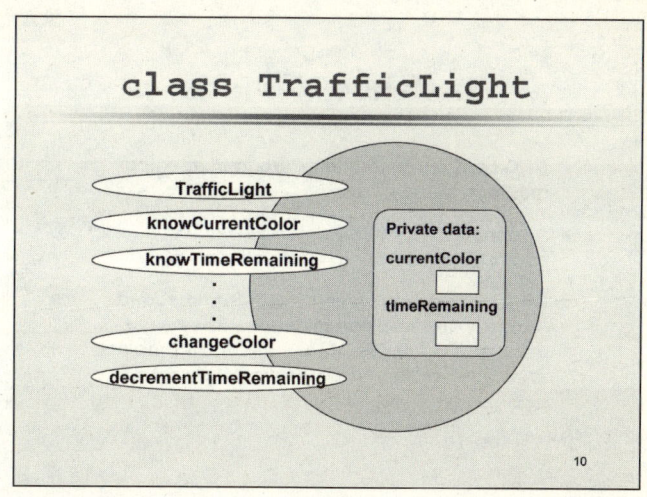

## Instance Methods

- CRC card responsibilities are implemented methods in the class.
- A responsibility that refers to an object should be implemented as an instance method.
- Constructors, observers, transformers, and iterators are instance methods. They have access to the fields of their associated object, and can receive values through the parameter list.

## Three Categories of Data

- **Instance data** is the internal representation of a specific object. It records the object's state.
- **Class data** is accessible to all objects of a class.
- **Local data** is specific to a given call of a method.

## Instance Data

**Instance data** is the internal representation of a specific object.

```
public class Name
{
    // Instance variables
    String first;
    String middle;
    String last;
    . . .
}
```

**Notes**

## Class Data

**Class data** is accessible to all objects of a class.
Fields declared as **static** belong to the class rather than to a specific instance.

```
public class Name
{
    // Class constant
    static final String PUNCT = ", ";
        . . .
}
```

## Local Data

**Local data** is specific to a given call of a method.
The JVM allocates space for this data when the method is called and deallocates it when the method returns.

```
public int compareTo(Name otherName)
{
  int result;    // Local variable
  . . .
    return  result;
}
```

## Lifetime

- **The lifetime of a variable, constant, or object is the** portion of an application's execution time when it is actually assigned space in memory.

## Lifetime of an Object

- When an object is instantiated using `new`, the JVM provides memory space for it from an area called the free pool or heap. The object's memory is deallocated (returned to the heap) when the JVM detects that no variable refers to it.

```
labelVar = new Label("One object");
labelVar = new Label("Another object");
```

## JVM's Garbage Collector

- Java contains an automatic garbage collector that periodically finds and returns to the heap any object that has no reference to it.

## Lifetime of Data

| CATEGORY | LIFETIME |
|---|---|
| Class | Execution of application program |
| Instance | From creation to destruction of its object |
| Local | From method call until return |

**Notes**

## Two Parts of Method Declaration

```
                heading
private static int square(int number)
{
    return  number * number ;        block
}
```

## Method Declaration Syntax

**MethodDeclaration**

Heading

Block

## What is in a block?

```
{

    0 or more statements here

}
```

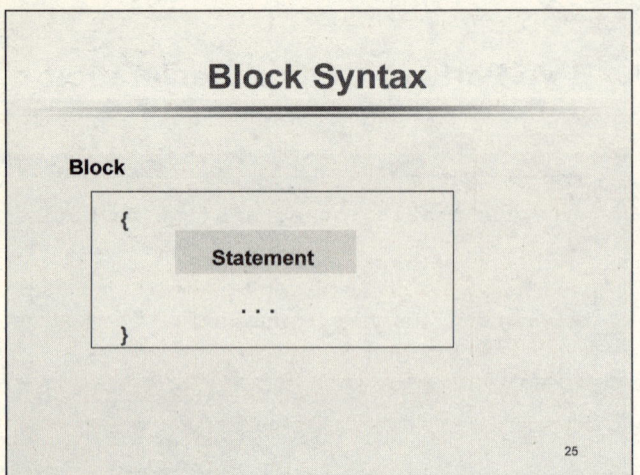

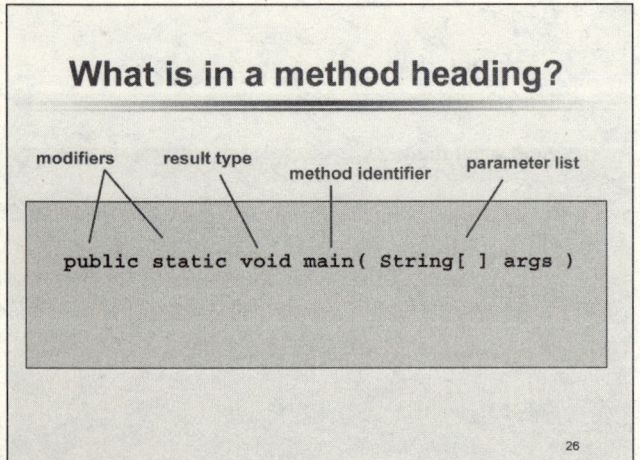

**Notes**

### Method Calls

A method is called by using the name of the method followed by ( ) enclosing a list of arguments.

```
System.out.println( "Done" );
a = Math.max( y, z );
value = Math.random( );
```

A method call temporarily transfers control to the called method to perform its task.

### Method Call Syntax

MethodName( Argument List )

The argument list is used to communicate values to the method by passing information.

The argument list can contain 0, 1, or more arguments, separated by commas, depending on the method.

### More about methods

- In Java, arguments should be used only for sending data into a method.
- Method calls are used to do tasks (implement responsibilities).
- Every Java method (except for constructors) has a result type.
- If the result type is not void, the method returns a value to the calling block.

## Method Call

- A method call temporarily transfers control to the called method's code.

- When the method's code has finished executing, control is transferred back to the calling block.

## When a method is called,

Temporary memory is set up (for its primitive data type arguments and any local variables, and also for the method's name if the return type is not void).

Then the flow of control passes to the first statement in the method's body. The called method's body statements are executed until one of these occurs:
 return statement (with or without a return value),
 or,
 closing brace of method body.

Then control goes back to where the method was called.

## A Java method can return

- in its identifier at most 1 value of the type specified (called the result type) in its heading.

- But, a void method cannot return any value in its identifier.

# Notes

## `return` Syntax

**ReturnStatement**

> return Expression ;

## `public` value-returning class method

```
public static int power ( int base , int exponent )
// Assumptions:  exponent is greater than or equal to 0.
//               base and exponent are not both zero
// Returns base raised to the exponent power.
{
    int  result ;       // Holds intermediate powers of base
    result = 1;
    while ( exponent > 0 ) {
        result = result * base ;
        exponent-- ;
    }
    return result ;
}
```

## `return;`

- is valid only in the body of void methods

- causes control to leave the method and immediately return to the calling block leaving any subsequent statements in the method body unexecuted.

## Parameter List

- is the means used for a method to share information with the block containing the call.

## Arguments are matched to parameters by their relative positions

```
// HEADING
public static int power ( int base , int exponent )
```

```
number = power ( 2 , 5 ) ;    // CALL
```

## Questions

- **Why is a method used?**
  To do a task (implement responsibilities).

- **Can one method call another method?**
  Yes

- **Can a method even call itself?**
  Yes, that is called recursion. It is very useful and requires special care in writing so that an infinite number of calls are not made.

**Notes**

## Methods are written to specifications (as on CRC card)

- The specifications state the result type, the parameter types, and what task the method is to perform using its parameters.

- The advantage is that teamwork can occur without knowing what the argument identifiers will actually be.

## Primitive and Reference Types

```
char letter ;
String title ;
String book ;
letter = 'J' ;
title = "Software Design";
book = title ;
```

Memory Location 2000

letter 'J'
title 2000
book 2000
→ "Software Design"

## Parameters in Java

- With **primitive data types** (such as int, double, boolean), the parameter receives a copy of the value of the argument. Operations on the parameter do not affect the argument.

- With **reference types** (such as String and other classes) the parameter receives a copy of the address where the object is stored. Making changes in the fields of the object referred to by the parameter does affect the argument object. *Doing so is poor programming practice.*

## Method mechanisms

| RESPONSIBILITY | SIMPLE TYPE | REFERENCE TYPE |
|---|---|---|
| Receives | Parameter | Parameter<br>*Instance method accesses field of object without changing* |
| Returns | `return` statement | `return` statement |
| Changes | `return` with replacement assignment after method returns | *Implement as instance method*<br>*Implement as class method* |

## ConstructorHeading Syntax

**ConstructorHeading**

Modifiers ClassIdentifier ( TypeName Identifier

, TypeName Identifier . . . )

## Package Syntax

**Package**

`package` Identifier ;

ImportDeclaration . . .

ClassDeclaration . . .

**Notes**

## Methods for Comparing Strings

| Method Name | Parameter Type | Returns | Operation Performed |
|---|---|---|---|
| equals | String | boolean | Tests for equality of string contents. |
| compareTo | String | int | Returns 0 if equal, a positive integer if the string in the parameter comes before the string associated with the method and a negative integer if the parameter comes after it. |

## `String` methods

| Method Name | Parameter Type | Returns | Operation Performed |
|---|---|---|---|
| toLowerCase | none | String | Returns a new identical string, except the characters are all lowercase. |
| toUpperCase | none | String | Returns a new identical string, except the characters are all uppercase. |

```java
// Code for package name
package name;
public class Name
{
    // Class constant
    static final String PUNCT = ", ";    // for formatting

    // Instance variables
    String first;
    String middle;
    String last;

    // Constructors
    public Name(String firstName, String middleName,
                String lastName)
    {
        first = firstName;
        middle = middleName;
        last = lastName;
    }
```

```
// package name     Continued

  // Basic Observers

  public String knowFirstName( )
  {
    return first;
  }

  public String knowMiddleName( )
  {
    return middle;
  }

  public String knowLastName( )
  {
    return last;
  }
```
49

```
// package name     Continued
  // More Observers

  public boolean equals(Name otherName)
  {
    return first.equals(otherName.first) &&
           middle.equals(otherName.middle) &&
           last.equals(otherName.last);
  }

  public String firstMidLast()
  {
    return   first + " " + middle + " " + last;
  }

  public String lastFirstMid()
  {
    return   last + PUNCT + first + " " + middle;
  }
```
50

```
// package name     Continued
  // Another Observer
  public int compareTo(Name otherName)
  {
    int result;
    result = last.toUpperCase().compareTo(
              otherName.last.toUpperCase());
    if (result != 0)
      return result;
    else
    {
      result = first.toUpperCase().compareTo(
                otherName.first.toUpperCase());
      if (result != 0)
        return result;
      else
        return middle.toUpperCase().compareTo(
                otherName.middle.toUpperCase());
    }
  }
}
```
51

# Notes

```java
// Driver for package name
import  name.*;
public class NameDriver
{
  static Name testName;     // Name object for testing
  static Name otherName;    // another Name object

  public static void main (String[ ] args)
  {
      System.out.println("Test Results for Package name");
      testName = new Name("John", "Kirk", "Herrel");
      // Observer tests
      System.out.println("Name      first     1     " +
        "John       " + testName.knowFirstName());
      System.out.println("Name      middle    1     " +
        "Kirk       " + testName.knowMiddleName());
      System.out.println("Name      last      1     " +
        "Herrel     " + testName.knowLastName());
```
52

```java
      // More observer tests
      otherName = new Name("John", "Kirk", "Herrel");
      System.out.println("Name      equals    1     " +
        "true       " + testName.equals(otherName));
      otherName = new Name("John", "Patrick", "Herrel");
      System.out.println("Name      equals    2     " +
        "false      " + testName.equals(otherName));
      otherName = new Name("John", "Kirk", "Herrel");
      System.out.println("Name      compareTo 1     " +
        "0          " + testName.compareTo(otherName));
      otherName = new Name("John", "Kirk", "Altman");
      System.out.println("Name      compareTo 2     " +
        "Positive int " + testName.compareTo(otherName));
      otherName = new Name("John", "Kirk", "Zigman");
      System.out.println("Name      compareTo 3     " +
        "Negative int " + testName.compareTo(otherName));
  }
}
```
53

# Chapter 8: Inheritance, Polymorphism, and Scope

### Slide 1

Introduction to
**Java and Software Design**

Dale • Weems • Headington

Chapter 8

Inheritance, Polymorphism, and Scope

### Slide 2

**Chapter 8 Topics**

- Inheritance and class hierarchy
- Overriding and hiding
- Polymorphism
- Scope of access rules
- Method signatures
- Method overloading
- Keywords `super` and `this`
- Shallow Copy vs. Deep Copy of Objects
- Meaning of a Copy Constructor

### Slide 3

**Inheritance hierarchy among vehicle classes**

Vehicle
├── WheeledVehicle
│   ├── Car
│   │   ├── TwoDoor
│   │   └── FourDoor
│   └── Bicycle
└── Boat

Every Car "is a" WheeledVehicle.

**Notes**

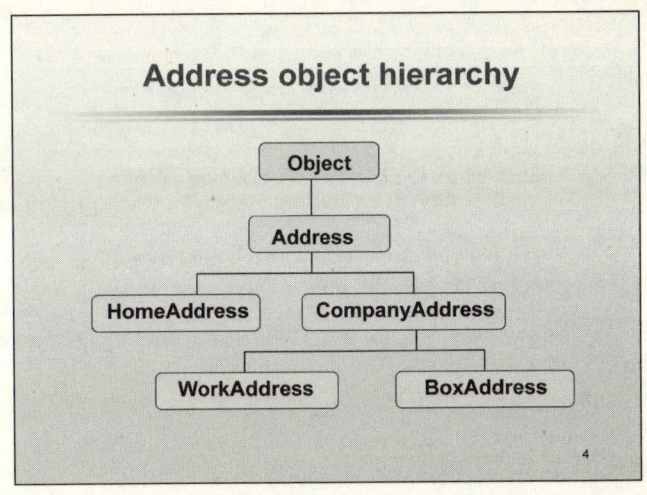

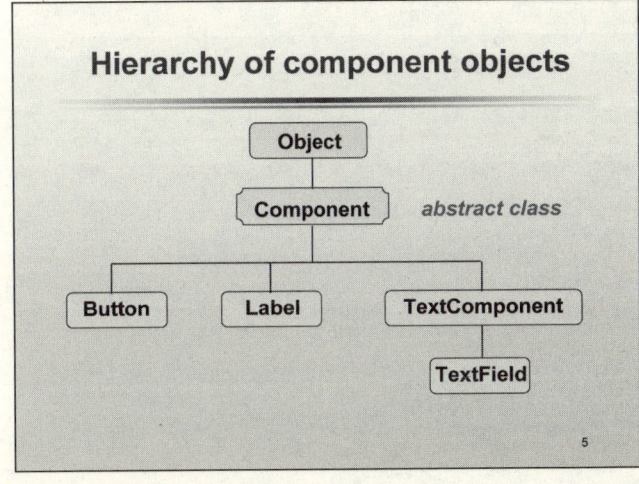

### Inheritance

- is a mechanism by which one class acquires (inherits) the properties (both data fields and methods) of another class.
- The class being inherited from is the superclass.
- The class that inherits is the subclass (derived class).
- The derived class is then specialized by adding properties specific to it.

## Inheritance

- Enables us to define a new class by adapting the definition of an existing class.

- The derived class is then specialized by adding properties specific to it.

## Hierarchy of component objects

```
          Object
            |
         Component
       /    |      \
   Button  Label  TextComponent
                       |
                   TextField
```

**WHAT ARE THE TextField INSTANCE METHODS?**

| TextField | TextComponent | *Component* | Object |
|---|---|---|---|
| TextField( ) | getSelectedText( ) | hide( ) | equals( Object obj) |
| TextField( int cols ) | getText( ) | show( ) | toString( ) |
| TextField( String text ) | setText( ) | isVisible( ) | . |
| TextField( String text, int cols) | paramString( ) | . | . |
| paramString( ) | . | . | |
| . | . | | |
| . | | | |

**Notes**

### Overriding vs. Hiding

- We *override* an instance method of a superclass by providing an instance method in a derived class with the same form of heading.

- We *hide* a data field of a superclass by providing a field in a derived class with the same name.

### Polymorphism

- Polymorphism is the ability of a language to have duplicate method names in an inheritance hierarchy and to decide which method is appropriate to call depending on the class of the object to which the method is applied.

### OOP Characteristics

| Characteristic | Meaning | Benefit |
| --- | --- | --- |
| Inheritance | New classes created from existing classes | Software resusabiltiy |
| Polymorphism | Write programs to handle variety of existing and future related classes | Add new capabilities |

## Class Syntax

Class

ClassModifier class Identifier extends ClassName
{
    ClassDeclaration
    ...
}

## Class Declaration Syntax

ClassDeclaration
- FieldDeclaration
- MethodDeclaration

## Scope of Identifier

- The scope of an identifier is the portion of program code where it is legal to use that identifier for any purpose.

# Notes

## Name precedence (or name hiding)

- A scope rule says that when a local identifier is declared with the same name as a class member, the class member is "hidden" until the block terminates execution.

- A hidden class member can be accessed by using keyword `this` together with the class member.

## Four Levels of Class Member Access

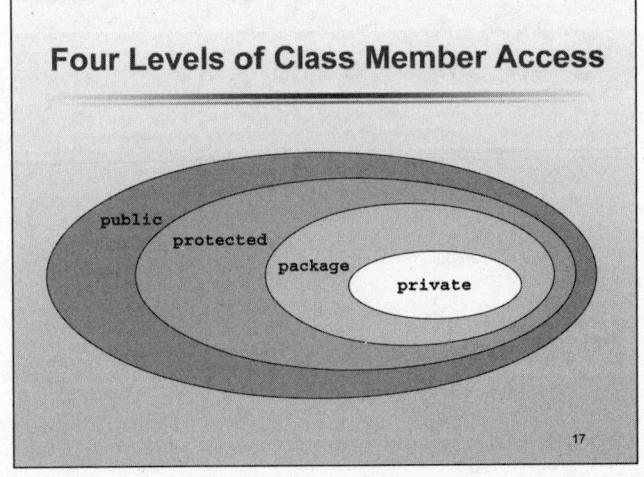

## Member Accessibility

| External access | public | protected | (default) package | private |
|---|---|---|---|---|
| Same package | yes | yes | yes | no |
| Derived class in another package | yes | yes (inheritance only) | no | no |
| User code | yes | no | no | no |

## Subclass Constructor

- **A subclass constructor always calls the superclass constructor first (either as a first statement call to `super`, or automatically when there is no call to `super`) to create and initialize members inherited from the superclass.**

## Method Signature

- The signature of a method consists of the method's name, **together with** the number and type(s) of its parameters in their given order.

- Method overloading is the use of a method name more than once, each time with different signatures.

## Method Overloading means

- **Several methods of the same name are defined with different sets of parameters (based on number of parameters, types of parameters, or order of parameters).**

# Notes

### class TextField constructors

```
//   Constructors
public TextField( )
//   Constructs a TextField object
public TextField( int columns )
//   Constructs a TextField with specified number of columns
public TextField( String s, int columns )
//   Constructs a TextField with text s in specified number
//   of columns
```

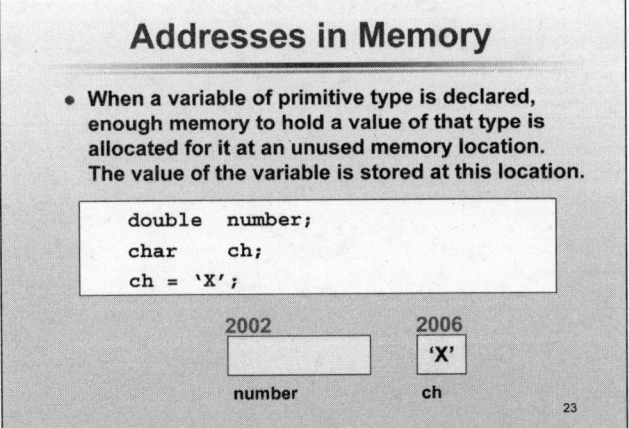

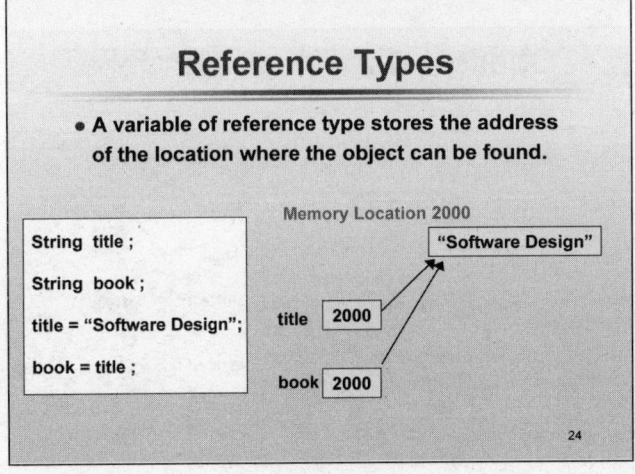

## class SavingsAccount

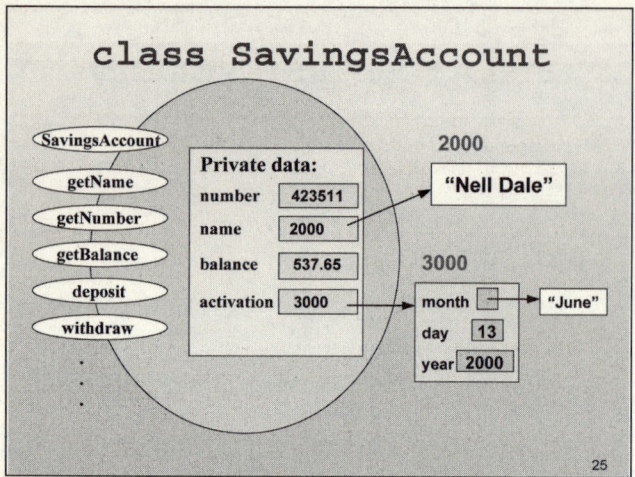

## Shallow Copy

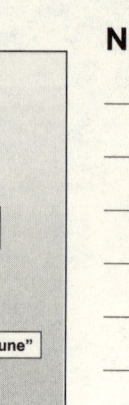

## Shallow Copy vs. Deep Copy

- *A shallow copy* copies all the class data fields, including references, and does not make a copy of any objects referred to by data fields.

- *A deep copy* copies the primitive type class data fields, and also makes a separately stored copy of what each reference refers to.

# Notes

## What's the difference?

- *A shallow copy* shares nested objects with the original class object.
- *A deep copy* makes its own copy of nested objects at different locations than in the original class object.

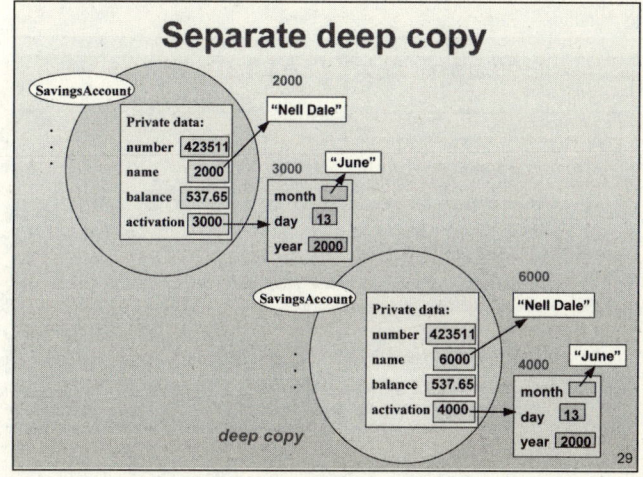

## Copy Constructor

- A copy constructor is a constructor that creates a deep copy of an object that can be used for other purposes, such as creating a new instance of an immutable object from an old one.

```
public SavingsAccount(SavingsAccount oldAcct,
                      String changeOfAddress)
{
    . . .          // create deep copy of oldAcct
}
```

```
// call
account = new Savings Account (oldAcct, newAddress)
```

## class `TextField` constructors

```
// Constructors

public TextField( )

// Constructs a TextField object

public TextField( int columns )

// Constructs a TextField with specified number of columns

public TextField( String s, int columns )

// Constructs a TextField with text s in specified number
// of columns
```

## class `TextField` methods

```
// Methods

public void setText( String s )

// Sets the text to be displayed in the TextField

public String getText( )

// Returns the string that the user has
// entered within the TextField

public String getSelectedText( )

// Returns the part of the string that the user has
// highlighted within the TextField
```

## TextField class

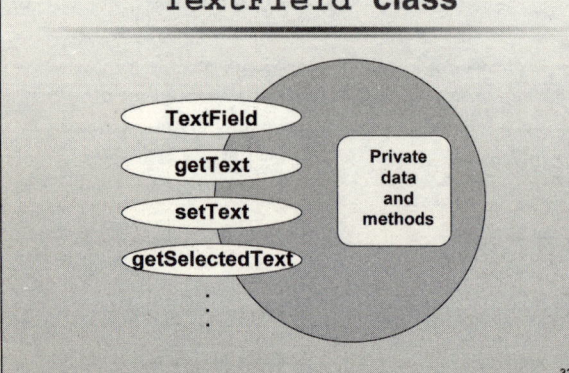

# Notes

```java
package numericField;
public class NumericField extends TextField
// This class provides a set of methods for directly getting
// and setting numeric values in a TextField derived object.
// It does not check for number format exceptions.  No
// TextField methods are overridden.  Only int and double are
// supported.
{
    // Constructors
    public NumericField( )
    {
        super( );
    }

    public NumericField( int columns )
    {
        super( columns );
    }
```

```java
    // More Constructors
    public NumericField( int value, int columns )
    {
        super( " " + value, columns );
    }

    public NumericField( double value, int columns )
    {
        super( " " + value, columns );
    }
    // Added methods
    public int getint( )
    {
        return Integer.valueOf(super.getText( )).intValue( );
    }

    public void setint( int value )
    {
        super.setText(" " + value );
    }
```

```java
    // More added methods
    public void getSelectedint( )
    {
        return Integer.valueOf(
                    super.getSelectedText( )).intValue( );
    }
    public int getdouble( )
    {
        return Double.valueOf(super.getText( )).doubleValue( );
    }

    public void setdouble( double value )
    {
        super.setText(" " + value );
    }

    public void getSelecteddouble( )
    {
        return Double.valueOf(
                    super.getSelectedText( )).doubleValue( );
    }
}
```

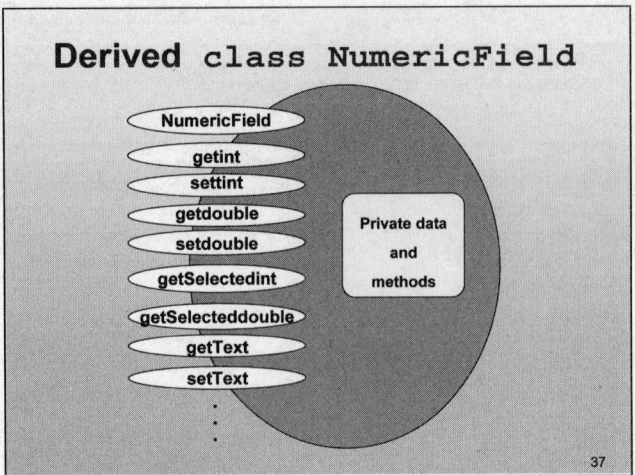

**Notes**

# Chapter 9: File I/O and Looping

**Notes**

## Introduction to Java and Software Design

Dale • Weems • Headington

Chapter 9

File I/O and Looping

## Chapter 9 Topics

- Using Data Files for I/O
- While Statement Syntax
- Count-Controlled Loops
- Event-Controlled Loops
- Using the End-of-File Condition
- Using a While Statement for Summing and Counting
- Nested While Loops
- Loop Testing and Debugging

## To Use File I/O, you must

- import package `java.io.*`
- choose valid identifiers and types for your file variables and declare them
- instantiate a file object for each file variable
- use your file identifiers in your I/O statements (using available methods such as read, skip, readLine, write, print, println)
- close the files when through

## What does instantiating a file do?

- associates the Java identifier for your file with the physical (disk) name for the file
- places a *file pointer* at the very beginning of the file, pointing to the first character in it
- if the output file does not exist on disk, an empty file with that name is created
- if the output file already exists, it is erased

## Using files for I/O

```
import.java.io.*;
```

input data → executing program → output data

disk file "myInfile.dat" — your variable (of type FileReader or BufferedReader)

disk file "myOutfile.dat" — your variable (of type FileWriter or PrintWriter)

## class FileReader

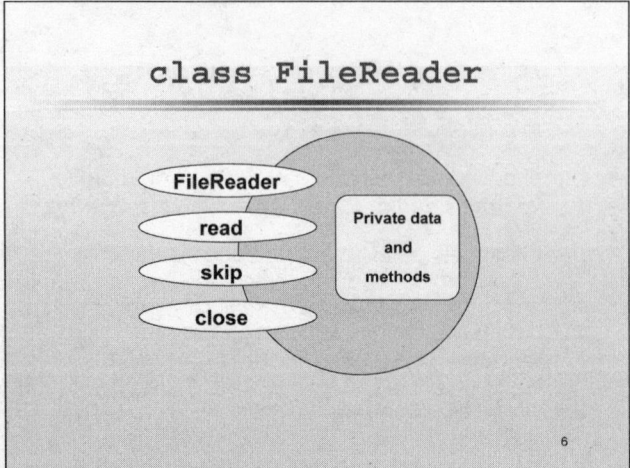

- FileReader
- read
- skip
- close

Private data and methods

**Notes**

# Notes

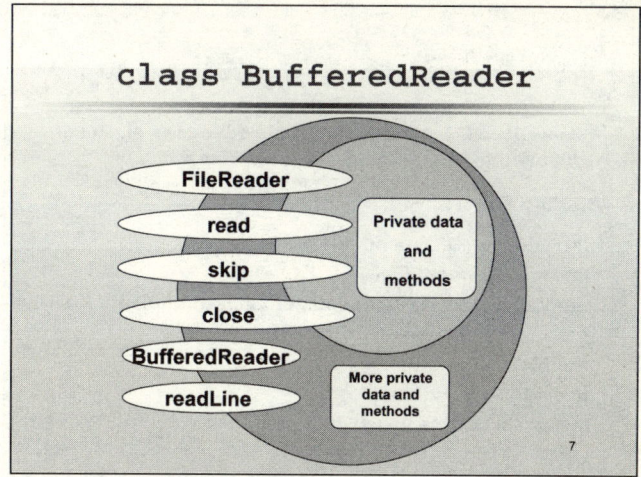

## readLine( ) method

- readLine( ) method of BufferedReader class uses no parameters and returns an object of class String.
- It reads a line of input from the file, including the end-of-line mark, but discards the EOL mark and stores the rest of the input line in the returned String.

EXAMPLE

String   line ;
line = inFile.readLine( ) ;

## readLine( )

- readLine reads successive characters (including blanks) into the string, and stops when it reaches the EOL, or newline mark '\n'.
- The newline is consumed by readLine, but is not stored into the returned String.

## readLine( ) method

- readLine( ) method of `BufferedReader` class can be used to input a numeric value from a file.

**EXAMPLES**

```
int   numberOfDependents;
line = inFile.readLine( );
numberOfDependents = Integer.valueOf(line).intValue( );
```

```
double   taxRate ;
line = inFile.readLine( );
taxRate = Double.valueOf( line ).doubleValue( );
```

---

```java
// Using Files
import java.io.*;              // File classes
public class EditLine {
    private static BufferedReader inFile; // Input data file
    private static PrintWriter outFile;   // Output data file

    public static void main( String[ ] args )
                                  throws IOException
    {
        // Prepare files for reading and writing
        inFile = new BufferedReader(
                         new FileReader("infile.dat"));
        outFile = new PrintWriter(
                         new FileWriter("outfile.dat"));
        . . .
        inFile.close( );
        outFile.close( );
    }
}
```

---

## class FileWriter

- FileWriter
- write
- flush
- close

Private data and methods

# Notes

## `write( )` method

- `write( )` method of `FileWriter` class can be passed a value of type `int` or a `String` object as parameter.
- An `int` parameter is first converted to the using Unicode and then written to the file as a character.

**EXAMPLE**

```
FileWriter outFile ;
outFile = new FileWriter("outfile.dat");
outFile.write('Q') ;
outFile.write("This is written to file.");
```

## class `PrintWriter`

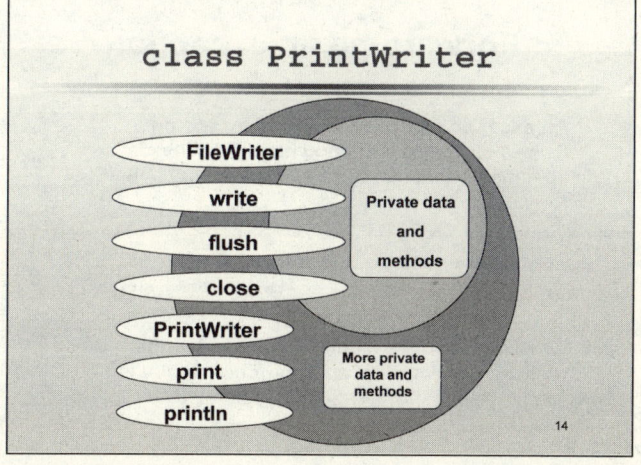

## `print( )` and `println( )` methods

- `print( )` method of `PrintWriter` class uses a parameter of any Java built-in data type (such as `char`, `int`, `long`, `float`, `double` or `String`).
- `println( )` automatically adds the EOL mark to the end of whatever it writes to the file.

**EXAMPLE**

```
PrintWriter  outFile ;
outFile = new PrintWriter( new FileWriter("outfile.dat") );
outFile.println( "Average blood pressure is " + avgBP
        + " for " + count + " patients." );
```

## What is an exception?

- An exception is an unusual situation detected while a program is running. It halts the normal execution of the method.

- Java recognizes two types of exceptions, checked and unchecked.

- Unchecked exceptions can be ignored, but checked exceptions must be explicitly recognized by the program.

## Forwarding an exception

- An exception can be forwarded by adding a throws clause to a method heading. The clause specifies the name of the exception that is being forwarded.

```
public static void main(String[ ] args)
                        throws IOException
```

- By doing so, the exception is passed to the method's caller, until an exception handler is found, or passing terminates with the JVM.

## `IOException`

- `FileReader`, `BufferedReader`, and `FileWriter` classes all throw an exception called `IOException`.

- `PrintWriter` methods do not throw any exceptions, but the `PrintWriter` constructor must be passed a `FileWriter` object that can throw an `IOException`.

**Notes**

**Notes**

### What is a loop?

- A loop is a repetition control structure.

- It causes a single statement or block to be executed repeatedly while an expression is true.

### Two types of loops

**count controlled loops**
repeat a specified number of times

**event-controlled loops**
something happens inside the loop body and this causes the repeating to stop

### while Statement

SYNTAX

```
while ( Expression )
{
    .
    .              // loop body
    .
}
```

NOTE: Loop body can be a single statement, a null statement, or a block.

When the expression is tested and found to be false, the loop is exited and control passes to the statement that follows the loop body.

## WHILE LOOP

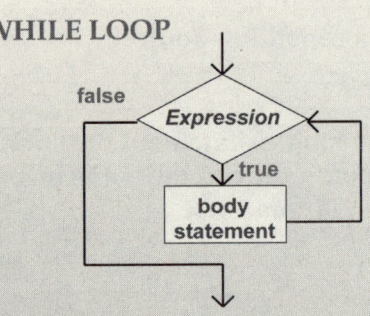

### Count-controlled loop contains

an initialization of the loop control variable

an expression to test for continuing the loop

an update of the loop control variable to be executed with each iteration of the body

### Count-controlled loop

```
int   loopCount ;
loopCount = 1;                  // initialize loop variable
while ( loopCount <= 10 )       // test expression
{
    .                           // repeated actions
    .
    .
    loopCount = loopCount + 1;  // update loop variable
}
```

**Notes**

### Count-controlled loop

```
int  count ;
count = 1;                          // initialize loop variable
while ( count <= 4 )  {             // test expression
                                    // repeated action
    System.out.println( "count is " + count );
    count ++ ;                      // update loop variable
}
System.out.println( "Done" );
```

### Count-controlled loop

```
int  count ;
count = 1;
while ( count <= 4 )  {
    System.out.println
        ( "count is " + count );
    count++ ;
}
System.out.println( "Done" );
```

count

OUTPUT

### Count-controlled loop

```
int  count ;
count = 1;
while ( count <= 4 )  {
    System.out.println
        ( "count is " + count );
    count++ ;
}
System.out.println( "Done" );
```

count

1

OUTPUT

## Count-controlled loop

```
int  count ;
count = 1;
while ( count <= 4 )  {      TRUE
    System.out.println
        ( "count is " + count );
        count++ ;
}
System.out.println( "Done" );
```

count: 1

OUTPUT:

## Count-controlled loop

```
int  count ;
count = 1;
while ( count <= 4 )  {
    System.out.println
        ( "count is " + count );
        count++ ;
}
System.out.println( "Done" );
```

count: 1

OUTPUT:
count is 1

## Count-controlled loop

```
int  count ;
count = 1;
while ( count <= 4 )  {
    System.out.println
        ( "count is " + count );
        count++ ;
}
System.out.println( "Done" );
```

count: 2

OUTPUT:
count is 1

**Notes**

### Count-controlled loop

```
int  count ;
count = 1;
while ( count <= 4 )  {      TRUE
   System.out.println
       ( "count is " + count );
   count++ ;
}
System.out.println( "Done" );
```

count
2

OUTPUT
count is 1

### Count-controlled loop

```
int  count ;
count = 1;
while ( count <= 4 )  {
   System.out.println
       ( "count is " + count );
   count++ ;
}
System.out.println( "Done" );
```

count
2

OUTPUT
count is 1
count is 2

### Count-controlled loop

```
int  count ;
count = 1;
while ( count <= 4 )  {
   System.out.println
       ( "count is " + count );
   count++ ;
}
System.out.println( "Done" );
```

count
3

OUTPUT
count is 1
count is 2

## Count-controlled loop

```
int count ;
count = 1;
while ( count <= 4 )  {     TRUE
    System.out.println
        ( "count is " + count );
    count++ ;
}
System.out.println( "Done" );
```

count: 3

OUTPUT
count is 1
count is 2

## Count-controlled loop

```
int count ;
count = 1;
while ( count <= 4 )  {
    System.out.println
        ( "count is " + count );
    count++ ;
}
System.out.println( "Done" );
```

count: 3

OUTPUT
count is 1
count is 2
count is 3

## Count-controlled loop

```
int count ;
count = 1;
while ( count <= 4 )  {
    System.out.println
        ( "count is " + count );
    count++ ;
}
System.out.println( "Done" );
```

count: 4

OUTPUT
count is 1
count is 2
count is 3

**Notes**

### Count-controlled loop

```
int count ;
count = 1;
while ( count <= 4 )  {    TRUE
   System.out.println
      ( "count is " + count );
   count++ ;
}
System.out.println( "Done" );
```

count
4

OUTPUT
count is 1
count is 2
count is 3

### Count-controlled loop

```
int count ;
count = 1;
while ( count <= 4 )  {
   System.out.println
      ( "count is " + count );
   count++ ;
}
System.out.println( "Done" );
```

count
4

OUTPUT
count is 1
count is 2
count is 3
count is 4

### Count-controlled loop

```
int count ;
count = 1;
while ( count <= 4 )  {
   System.out.println
      ( "count is " + count );
   count++ ;
}
System.out.println( "Done" );
```

count
5

OUTPUT
count is 1
count is 2
count is 3
count is 4

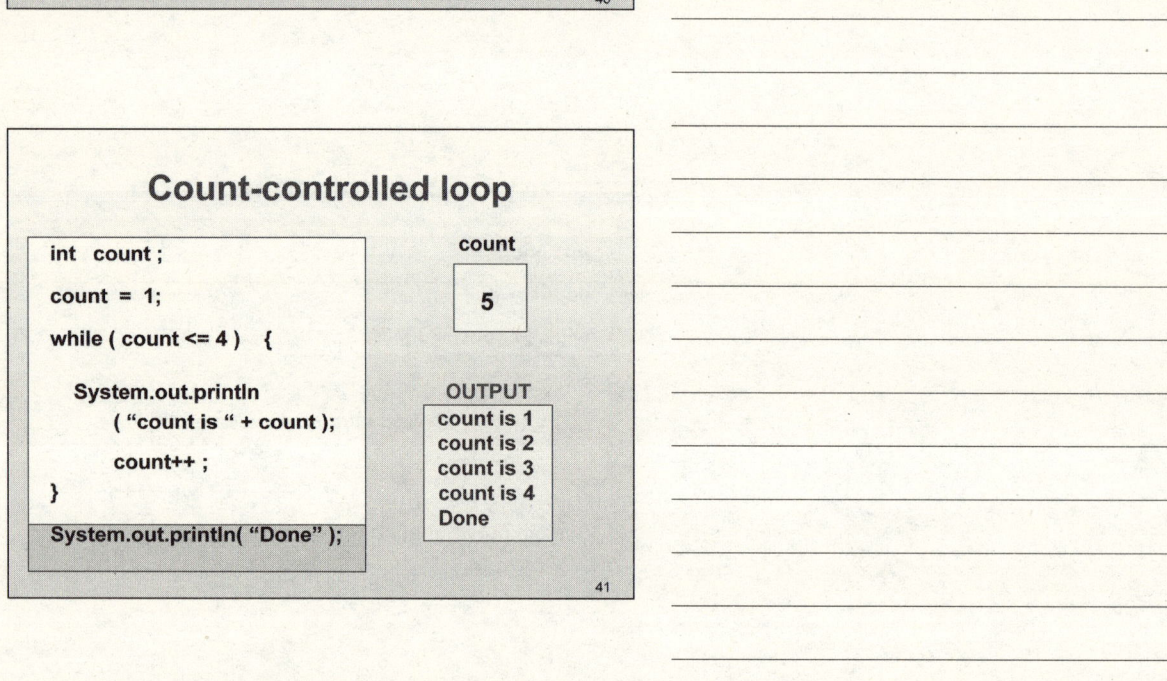

# Notes

```java
// Count-controlled loop
int    thisBP ;
int    total ;
int    count ;

count = 1 ;                              // initialize
total = 0;
while  ( count <= 100 )                  // test expression
{
   thisBP =
       Integer.valueOf( dataFile.readLine( ) ).intValue( ) ;

   total = total + thisBP ;
   count++ ;                             // update
}
System.out.println("The total = " + total ) ;
```

## Event-controlled loops

- **Sentinel controlled**
  keep processing data until a special value which is not a possible data value is entered to indicate that processing should stop.

- **End-of-file controlled**
  keep processing data as long as there is more data in the file.

- **Flag controlled**
  keep processing data until the value of a flag changes in the loop body.

## Examples of kinds of loops

| | |
|---|---|
| Count controlled loop | Read exactly 100 blood pressures from a file. |
| End-of-file controlled loop | Read all the blood pressures from a file no matter how many are there. |
| Flag controlled loop | Read blood pressures until a dangerously high BP (200 or more) is read. |

## A Sentinel-controlled loop

- Requires a "priming read"

- "Priming read" means you read one set of data before entering the while loop

## Using '\n' as sentinel value

```
// Sentinel controlled loop to read all the characters
// on an input line and print them to an output file.
char  inChar;
. . .
inChar = (char) inFile.read( ) ;    // Get first character
while ( inChar != '\n' )            // while not sentinel
{
    outFile.write( inChar );
    inChar = (char) inFile.read( ) ;  // Get next character
}
```

## End-of-File controlled loop

- **depends on fact that each method has its own sentinel value (-1 for `read`, `null` for `readLine`) to return to signal that the end of the file has been reached.**

**Notes**

```
// End-of-file controlled loop
int     thisBP ;
int     total ;
int     count ;

count = 1 ;                              // initialize
total = 0;

line = dataFile.readLine( );             // priming read
while   ( line != null )     // while last read successful
{
   thisBP = Integer.valueOf( line ).intValue( ) ;
   total = total + thisBP ;
   count++ ;                             // update
   line = dataFile.readLine( );          // read another
}
System.out.println("The total = " + total ) ;
```

## Flag-controlled loops

- Use meaningful name for the flag
- You initialize flag (to true or false)
- Test for the flag in the loop test expression
- A condition in the loop body changes the value of the flag

## Using a flag-controlled loop

- to count and sum the first 10 odd numbers in a data file
  - flag `notDone` is initialized to `true`
  - loop test will be `while (notDone)`
  - flag value will be changed to `false` if 10 odd numbers have been read, or if EOF is reached unexpectedly

```
count = 0;               // initialize event counter
sum = 0;                 // initialize sum
notDone = true;          // initialize loop control flag
while ( notDone )
{
   line = dataFile.readLine( ); // get a line
   if ( line != null )          // got a line?
   {
      number = Integer.valueOf(line).intValue( );
      if ( number % 2 == 1 )    // is number odd?
      {
         count++;               // increment count
         sum = sum + number;    // add number to sum
         notDone = ( count < 10 );  // update flag
      }
   }
   else                         // reached EOF unexpectedly
   {
      errorFile.println("EOF reached before ten odd values.")
      notDone = false;          // change flag value
   }
}
```
52

## Loops often used to

- **Count all data values**
- **Count special data values**
- **Sum data values**

53

```
// Flag and EOF controlled loop

countGoodReadings = 0;              // initialize
isSafe = true;

while (isSafe && (line = dataFile.readLine() != null))
{
   thisBP = Integer.valueOf(line).intValue( );
   if   ( thisBP >=  200 )
       isSafe = false;              // change flag
   else
       countGoodReadings++;         // update
   }
}

System.out.println("There were " + countGoodReadings
                + " safe blood pressure readings.")
```
54

# Notes

### Pattern of a nested loop

```
initialize outer loop
while ( outer loop condition )
{     . . .
      initialize inner loop
      while ( inner loop condition )
      {
            inner loop processing and update
      }
      . . .
}
```

### To design a nested loop

- Begin with outer loop.

- When you get to where the inner loop appears, make it a separate module and come back to its design later.

### Algorithm uses Nested Loops

- get a data line from the data file
- while the end of data file has not been reached
    - obtain starCount from the data line
    - use a count-controlled loop to print starCount asterisks to the output file
    - print a newline character to the output file
    - read next data line from the data file
- print "End" to the output file

The Student Lecture Companion

```
// Using nested loops
line = dataFile.readLine( );        // get data line
while ( line != null )              // while not end-of-file
{
    starCount = Integer.valueOf(line).intValue( );
    loopCount = 1;                  // loop to print asterisks
    while ( loopCount <= starCount )
    {
        outFile.print('*');
        loopCount ++;
    }
    outFile.println( );
    line = dataFile.readLine( );    // get next data line
}
outFile.println("End");
```

## Information about 20 books in file

Hardback or Paperback?    bookfile.dat    Price of book

```
P  3.98
H  7.41
P  8.79
```

WRITE A PROGRAM TO FIND TOTAL VALUE OF ALL BOOKS

## Loop to read information about 20 books from a file

```
String    line;    // declarations
String    kind ;
double    price ;
double    total  = 0.0 ;
int       count  = 1;
             . . .
while ( ( line = dataFile.readLine( ) ) && count <= 20 )
{
    kind = line.substring(0, 1);
    price = Double.valueOf(
            line.substring(1, line.length( ) ) ).doubleValue( );
    total = total + price ;
    count ++ ;
}
```

**Notes**

## Trace of Program Variables

| count | kind | price | total |
|---|---|---|---|
|  |  |  | 0.0 |
| 1 | "P" | 3.98 | 3.98 |
| 2 | "H" | 7.41 | 11.39 |
| 3 | "P" | 8.79 | 20.18 |
| 4 | etc. |  |  |
|  |  |  |  |
| 20 |  |  |  |
| 21 | so loop terminates |  |  |

## Complexity

- is a measure of the amount of work involved in executing an algorithm relative to the size of the problem.

## Order of Magnitude of a Function

The **order of magnitude**, or **Big-O notation**, of an expression describes the complexity of an algorithm according to the highest order of N that appears in its complexity expression.

## Names of Orders of Magnitude

$O(1)$       constant time

$O(\log_2 N)$       logarithmic time

$O(N)$       linear time

$O(N^2)$       quadratic time

$O(N^3)$       cubic time

## Polynomial Times

| N | $N^0$ constant | $N^1$ linear | $N^2$ quadratic | $N^3$ cubic |
|---|---|---|---|---|
| 1 | 1 | 1 | 1 | 1 |
| 10 | 1 | 10 | 100 | 1,000 |
| 100 | 1 | 100 | 10,000 | 1,000,000 |
| 1,000 | 1 | 1,000 | 1,000,000 | 1,000,000,000 |
| 10,000 | 1 | 10,000 | 100,000,000 | 1,000,000,000,000 |

## Loop Testing and Debugging

- Test data should test all sections of program
- Beware of infinite loops -- program doesn't stop.
- Check loop termination condition, and watch for "off-by-1" problem.
- Use `read` method for loops controlled by detection of '\n' character.
- Use algorithm walk-through to verify that appropriate conditions occur in the right places.
- Trace execution of loop by hand with code walk-through.
- Use a debugger (if available) to run program in "slow motion" or use debug output statements.

## Notes

### `incomes.dat`

- A file contains income data for different people.
- Each line has an M or F for gender, followed by the salary amount for that person

gender   amount

| | |
|---|---|
| M | 38119.29 |
| F | 24345.23 |
| F | 32933.73 |
| M | 31820.04 |

### results.dat

For 6 females, the average income is 37097.99667.
For 2 males, the average income is 47067.51250.

### Incomes CRC Card

| Class Name: Incomes | Superclass: Object | Subclasses: |
|---|---|---|
| **Responsibilities** | **Collaborations** ||
| Prepare the file for input | FileReader, BufferedReader ||
| Prepare the file for output | FileWriter, PrintWriter ||
| Calculate the averages | BufferedReader ||
| Write results to file | PrintWriter ||

```
// Reads a file of income amounts classified by gender
// and computes the average income for each gender.

import    java.io.*;                     // File types

public class Incomes {

    public static void main( String[ ] args )
                                        throws IOException
    {
        int    femaleCount;
        double femaleSum;
        double femaleAvg;
        int    maleCount;
        double maleSum;
        double maleAvg;
        String inLine;
        char   gender;
```

70

```
        String   amountString;
        double   amount;
        BufferedReader  inFile;
        PrintWriter outFile;
        // Prepare files for reading and writing
        inFile = new BufferedReader(
                            new FileReader("gender.dat"));
        outFile = new PrintWriter(
                            new FileWriter("results.dat"));
        // Initialize process
        femaleCount = 0;
        femaleSum = 0.0;
        maleCount = 0;
        maleSum = 0.0;
```

71

```
        // Calculate averages
        while  ( (inLine = inFile.readLine( ) ) != null )
        {
                        // Gender is first character
            gender = inLine.charAt(0);
                        // Amount begins in third position
            amountString = inLine.substring(2, inLine.length( ));
            amount = Double.valueOf(amountString).doubleValue( );
            // Process based on gender code
            if ( gender == 'F' )
            {
                femaleCount++;
                femaleSum = femaleSum + amount;
            }
            else
            {
                maleCount++;
                maleSum = maleSum + amount;
            }
        }
```

72

# Notes

```java
        // Compute average incomes
        femaleAvg = femaleSum / (double)femaleCount;
        maleAvg = femaleSum / (double)femaleCount;

        // Write results to outFile

        outFile.println( "For " + femaleCount
                    + " females, the average income is "
                    + femaleAvg + "." );

        outFile.println( "For " + maleCount
                    + " males, the average income is "
                    + maleAvg + "." );

        inFile.close( );
        outFile.close( );
    }
}
```

# Chapter 10: Additional Control Structures and Exceptions

## Introduction to Java and Software Design

Dale • Weems • Headington

Chapter 10

Additional Control Structures and Exceptions

## Chapter 10 Topics

- `switch` Multiway Branching Structure
- `do` Statement for Looping
- `for` Statement for Looping
- `break` Statement
- Bitwise Logical Operators
- Ternary and Assignment Operators
- Exception Handling using `try` and `catch`
- Defining Exception Classes

## `Switch` Statement

Is a selection control structure for multiway branching.

SYNTAX

```
switch ( IntegralExpression ) {

    case Constant1 :
        Statement(s);        // optional
    case Constant2 :
        Statement(s);        // optional
        .
        .
    default :                // optional
        Statement(s);        // optional
}
```

# Notes

```java
double  weightInPounds = 165.8 ;
char    weightUnit ;
        . . .              // obtain letter for desired weightUnit
switch ( weightUnit ) {
    case 'P' :  case 'p' :
        System.out.println( "Weight in pounds is " + weightInPounds );
        break ;
    case 'O' :  case 'o' :
        System.out.println( "Weight in ounces is " + 16.0 * weightInPounds );
        break ;
    case 'K' :  case 'k' :
        System.out.println( "Weight in kilos is " + weightInPounds / 2.2 );
        break ;
    case 'G' :  case 'g' :
        System.out.println( "Weight in grams is " + 454.0 * weightInPounds );
        break ;
    default :
        System.out.println( "That unit is not handled!" );
        break ;
}
```

## `switch` Structure

- The value of *IntegralExpression* (of byte, char, short, or int type ) determines which branch is executed.

- Case labels are constant ( possibly named ) integral expressions. Several case labels can precede a statement.

## Control in `switch` Structure

- Control branches to the statement following the case label that matches the value of *IntegralExpression*. Control proceeds through all remaining statements, including the default, unless redirected with break.

- If no case label matches the value of *IntegralExpression*, control branches to the default label, if present. Otherwise control passes to the statement following the entire switch structure.

- Forgetting to use break can cause logical errors because after a branch is taken, control proceeds sequentially until either break or the end of the switch structure occurs.

## break Statement

- break statement can be used with switch or any of the 3 looping control structures.

- It causes an immediate exit from the switch, while, do, or for statement in which it appears.

- If the break is inside nested structures, control exits only the innermost structure containing it.

## Count-controlled loop requires:

1. The name of a control variable (or loop counter).

2. The initial value of the control variable.

3. The increment (or decrement) by which the control variable is modified each time through the loop.

4. The condition that tests for the final value of the control variable (to determine if looping should continue).

## do Statement Syntax

Is a looping control structure in which the loop condition is tested *after* executing the body of the loop.

**DoStatement**

```
do
    Statement
while ( Expression ) ;
```

Loop body can be a single statement or a block.

**Notes**

# Notes

### Using `do` to implement a count-controlled loop

```
// Count-controlled repetition

    sum = 0;                        // initialize
    counter = 1;

    do
    {
        sum = sum + counter;
        counter++;                  // increment
    } while ( counter <= 10 );      // condition
```

### `do` vs. `while`

- POSTTEST loop (exit-condition)
- The loop condition is tested after executing the loop body.
- Loop body is always executed at least once.

- PRETEST loop (entry-condition)
- The loop condition is tested before executing the loop body.
- Loop body may not be executed at all.

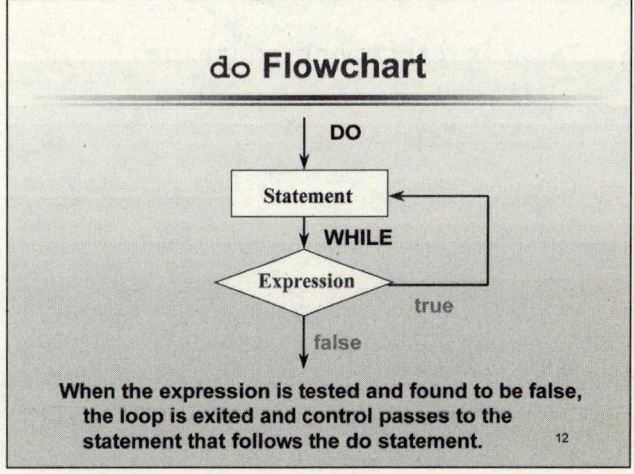

### `do` Flowchart

When the expression is tested and found to be false, the loop is exited and control passes to the statement that follows the do statement.

## for Statement Syntax

**ForStatement**

for ( Init ; Expression ; Update )
    Statement

## A Count-Controlled Loop

**SYNTAX**

for ( *initialization* ; *test expression* ; *update* ) {
    0 or more statements to repeat
}

## The for statement contains

an Initialization

a boolean Expression to test for continuing

an Update to execute after each iteration of the loop body

## Notes

### Example of Repetition

```
int num;

for ( num = 1 ;  num <= 3 ;  num++ ) {

    System.out.println( "Potato " + num );
}
```

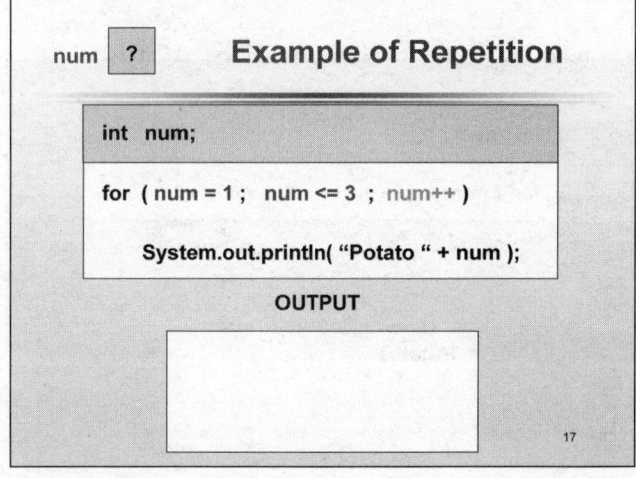

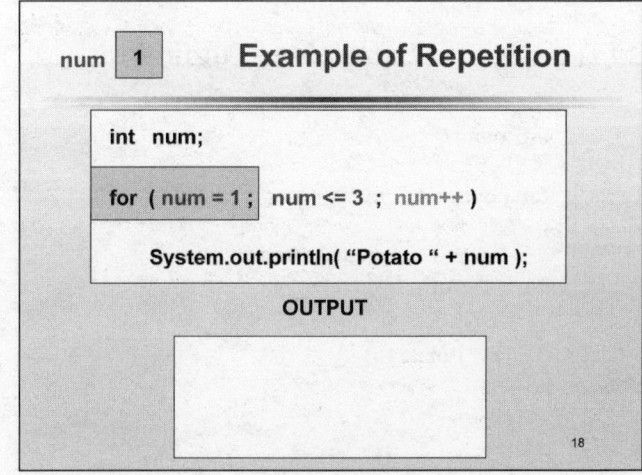

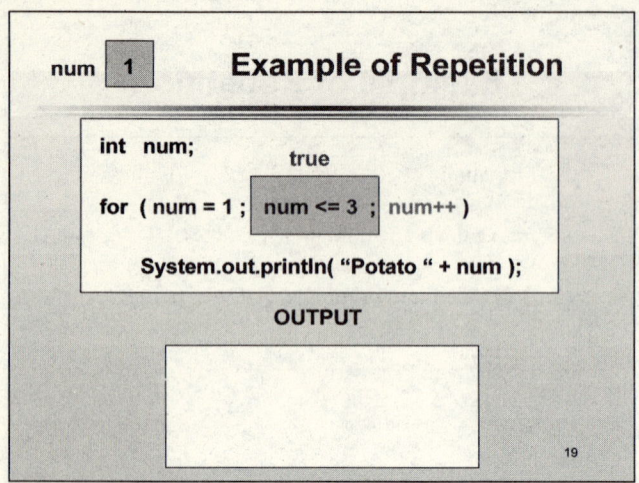

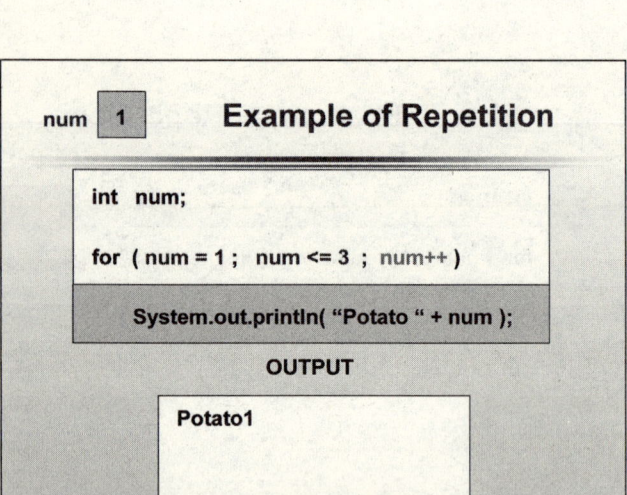

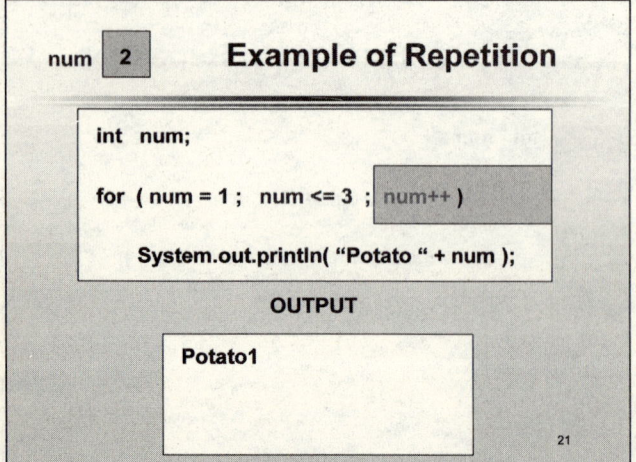

# Notes

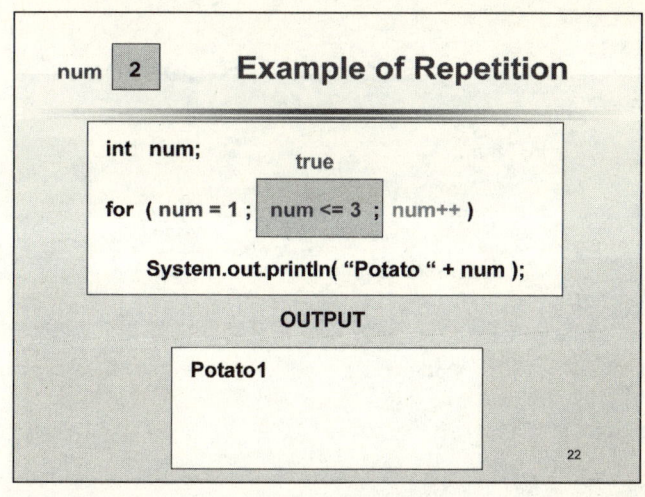

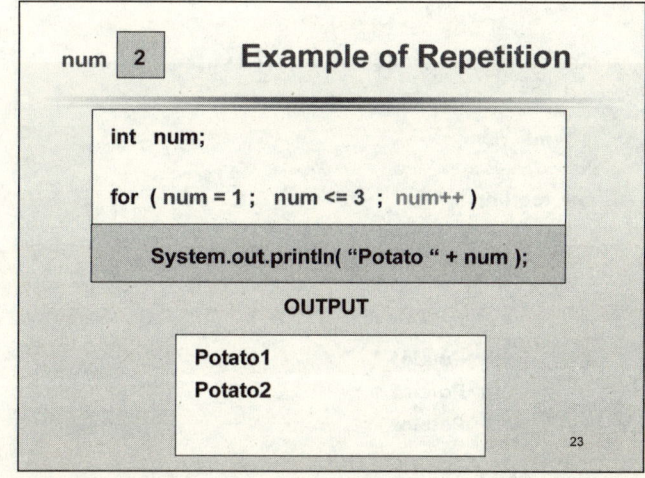

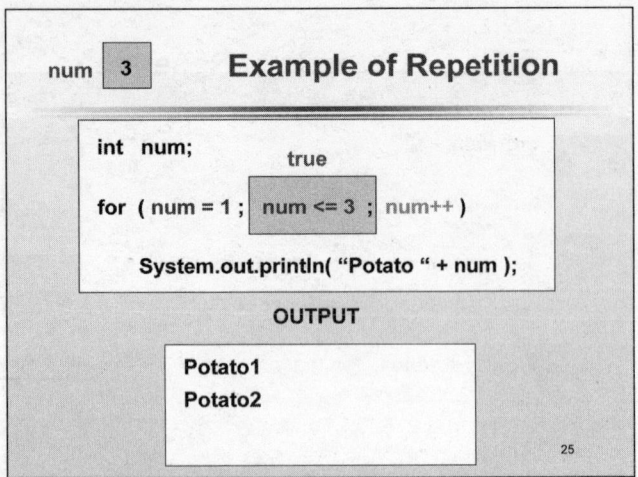

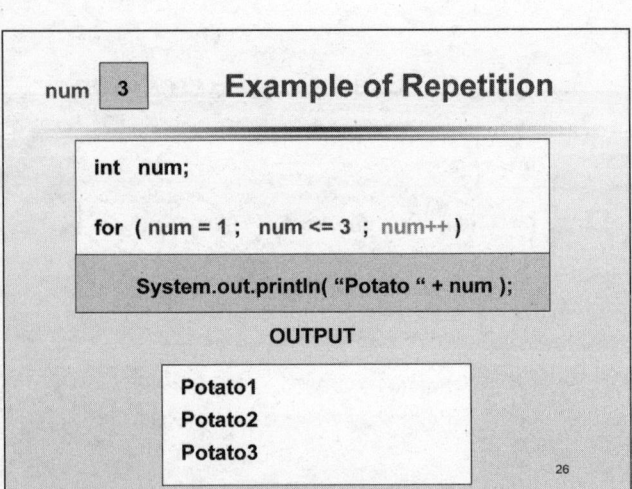

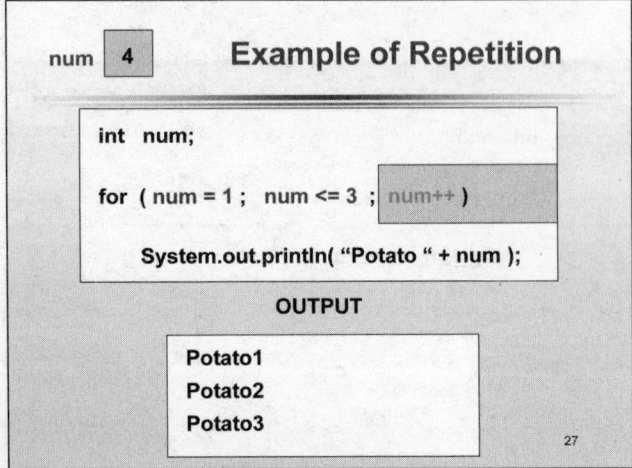

**Notes**

**Notes**

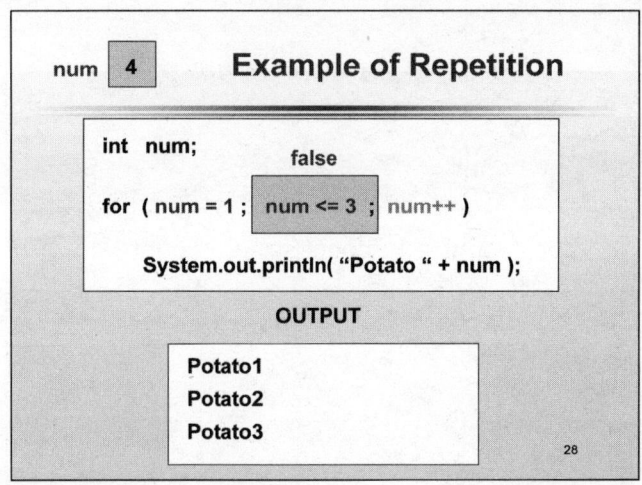

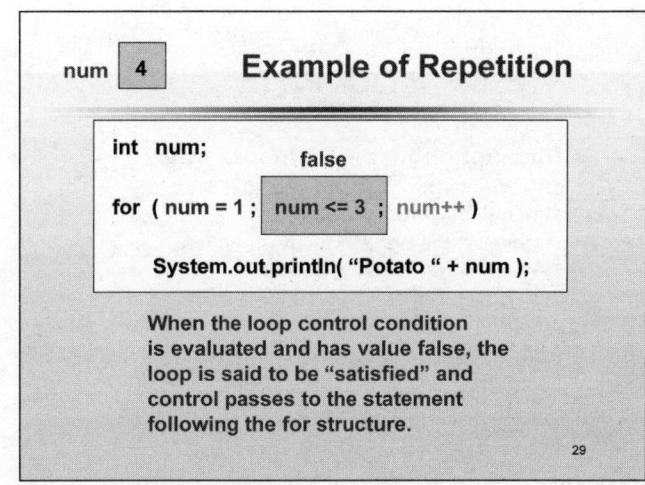

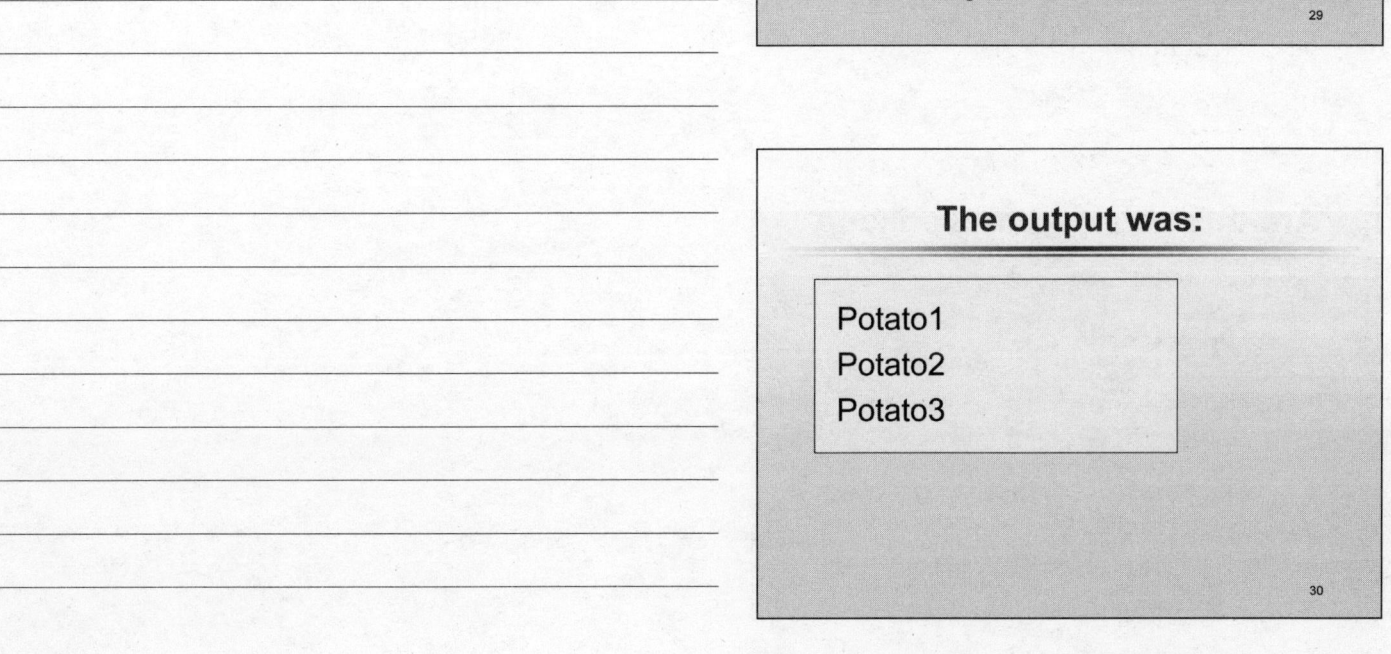

## What output from this loop?

```
int count;

for (count = 1; count <= 10; count++) ;

    System.out.println( "*" );
```

## OUTPUT

- **No output from the for loop! Why?**
- The ; right after the ( ) means that the body statement is a null statement
- In general, the body of the for loop is whatever statement *immediately* follows the ( )
- That statement can be a single statement, a compound statement, or a null statement.
- Actually, the code outputs one * after the loop completes its counting from 1 to 11.

## Another count-controlled loop

```
//  Calculating compound interest
    double amount;
    double principal = 1000.0;
    double rate = 0.07;

    System.out.println("Year      Amount");

    for ( int year = 1; year <= 10; year++ )
    {
        amount = principal * Math.pow( 1.0 + rate, year );
        System.out.println(year + " " + amount);
    }
```

# Notes

## Java Has Combined Assignment Operators

```
int age ;
```

Write a statement to add 3 to age.

```
age = age + 3 ;
```
OR,
```
age += 3 ;
```

---

Write a statement to subtract 10 from `weight`

```
int weight ;
```

```
weight = weight - 10 ;
```
OR,
```
weight -= 10 ;
```

---

Write a statement to divide `money` by 5.0

```
double money ;
```

```
money = money / 5.0 ;
```
OR,
```
money /= 5.0 ;
```

**Write a statement to double `profits`**

```
double  profits ;
```

```
profits  =  profits * 2.0 ;
```
OR,
```
profits  *=  2.0 ;
```

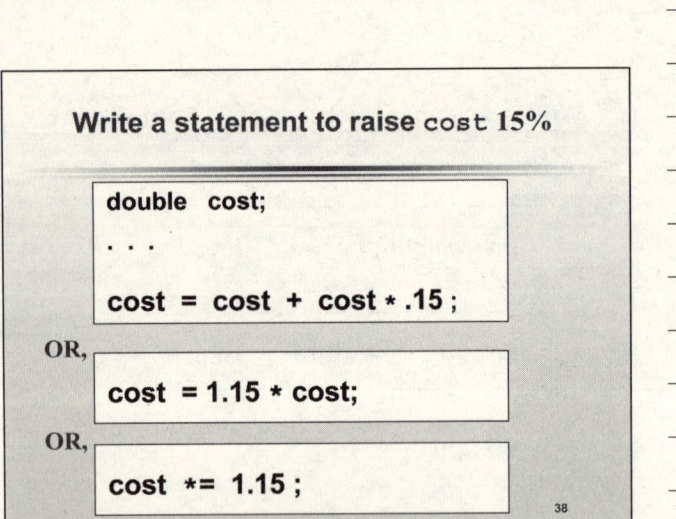

**Write a statement to raise `cost` 15%**

```
double  cost;
. . .
cost  =  cost  +  cost * .15 ;
```
OR,
```
cost  =  1.15 * cost;
```
OR,
```
cost  *=  1.15 ;
```

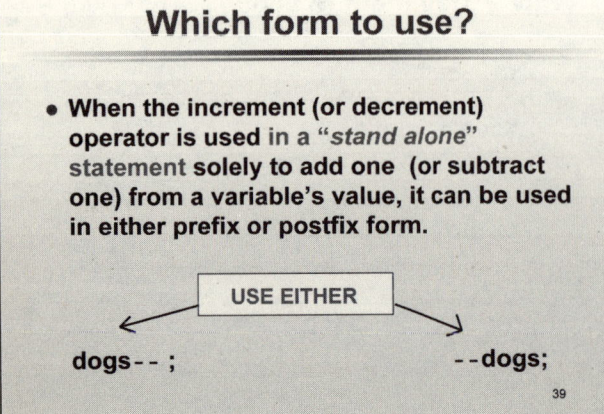

## Which form to use?

- When the increment (or decrement) operator is used in a *"stand alone"* statement solely to add one (or subtract one) from a variable's value, it can be used in either prefix or postfix form.

USE EITHER

dogs-- ;          --dogs;

**Notes**

---

## BUT...

- When the increment (or decrement) operator is used in a statement with other operators, the prefix and postfix forms can yield *different* results.

  LET'S SEE HOW...

40

---

## PREFIX FORM
### "First increment, then use"

```
int alpha ;
int num ;

num = 13;

alpha = ++num * 3;
```

| 13 | |
|---|---|
| num | alpha |

| 14 |
|---|
| num |

| 14 | 42 |
|---|---|
| num | alpha |

41

---

## POSTFIX FORM
### "Use, then increment"

```
int alpha ;
int num ;

num = 13;

alpha = num++  * 3;
```

| 13 | |
|---|---|
| num | alpha |

| 13 | 39 |
|---|---|
| num | alpha |

| 14 |
|---|
| num |

42

## Operators can be

| | | |
|---|---|---|
| binary | involving 2 operands | 2 + 3 |
| unary | involving 1 operand | - 3 |
| ternary | involving 3 operands | *follows* |

## Conditional (Ternary) Operator
### ? :

**SYNTAX**

> *Expression1* ? *Expression2* : *Expression3*

**MEANING**

If *Expression1* is true, then the value of the entire expression is *Expression2*. Otherwise, the value of the entire expression is *Expression 3*.

FOR EXAMPLE . . .

## Using Conditional Operator

```
// Finds the smaller of two float values

    double   min ;
    double   x ;
    double   y ;

    . . .

    min = ( x < y ) ? x : y ;
```

**Notes**

## Control Structures

**Use logical expressions which may include:**

*6 Relational Operators*

    <    <=    >    >=    ==    !=

*6 Logical Operators*

    !    &&    ||    ^    &    |

| LOGICAL EXPRESSION | MEANING | DESCRIPTION |
|---|---|---|
| p \| q | Bitwise logical inclusive OR | p \| q is false if both p and q are false. It is true otherwise. |
| p & q | Bitwise logical AND | p & q is true if both p and q are true. It is false otherwise. |
| p ^ q | Bitwise logical exclusive OR | p ^ q is true only if p and q have different boolean values. It is false otherwise. |

## Short-Circuit Evaluation

- Java uses short circuit evaluation of logical expressions involving && and ||.

- This means logical expressions with && and || are evaluated left to right and evaluation stops as soon as the correct boolean value of the entire expression is known.

- Expressions involving & and | work identically to those involving && and || with the exception that both operands are always evaluated (there is no short-circuit evaluation).

## Precedence (highest to lowest)

| Operator | Associativity |
|---|---|
| ( ) | Left to right |
| unary: ++ -- ! + - (cast) | Right to left |
| * / % | Left to right |
| + - | Left to right |
| < <= > >= | Left to right |
| == != & | Left to right |
| ^ | Left to right |
| \| | Left to right |
| && | Left to right |
| \|\| | Left to right |
| ? : | Right to left |
| = += -= *= /= | Right to left |

## try-catch-finally

```
try
{
    . . .     // Statements that try to open a file
}
catch (IOException except)
{
    . . .     // Statements execute if can't open file
}
finally
{
    . . .     // Statements are always executed
}
```

## try-catch Example

```
filename = fileField.getText( );

try
{
    outFile = new PrintWeriter(new FileWriter(filename));
}
catch (IOException except)
{
    errorLabel.setText("Unable to open file " + filename);
    fileField.setText("");
}
```

**Notes**

## Three Part Exception Handling

- Defining the exception
    By extending type Exception and supplying a pair of constructors that call super

- Raising (generating) the exception
    By use of the throw statement

- Handling the exception
    By use of a throws clause specifying the type of exception being forwarded
    or,
    By use of try-catch-finally to catch an exception.

## Rainfall CRC Card

| Class Name: Incomes | Superclass: Object | Subclasses: |
|---|---|---|
| **Responsibilities** | **Collaborations** ||
| Prepare the file for input | FileReader, BufferedReader ||
| Prepare the file for output | FileWriter, PrintWriter ||
| Process data | BufferedReader ||
| Throw exceptions if necessary | DataSetException ||

## Defining an Exception Class

```
//   Defines an Exception class for signaling data set errors
package   rainfall;
class DataSetException extends Exception
{
  public DataSetException( )
  {
      super( );
  }

  public DataSetException( String message )
  {
      super( message );
  }
}
```

```
// Inputs 12 monthly rainfall amounts from a file and
// computes the average monthly rainfall.  This process
// is repeated for any number of recording sites.
package  rainfall;
import   java.io.*;

public class Rainfall
{
  static void processOneSite( BufferedReader infile,
           PrintWriter outFile, String dataSetName )
  {
    int    count;              // Loop control variable
    double amount;             // Rain for one month
    double sum = 0.0;          // Sums annual rainfall
    String dataLine;           // Input from inFile
    String currentValue;       // String for numeric
    int    index;              // Position of blank

    try
    {                          // Could produce an IOException
      dataLine = inFile.readLine( );
```
55

```
    for (count = 1; cout <= 12; count++)
    {                          // Find position of blank
      index = dataLine.indexOf(' ');
      if (index > 0)
      {                        // Blank found
        currentValue = dataLine.substring(0, index);
        dataLine = dataLine.substring(
                 Math.min(index+1, dataLine.length()),
                 dataLine.length( ));
      }
      else   // Remaining string is current value
        currentValue = dataLine;
      amount = Double.valueOf
                       (currentValue).doubleValue( );
      if (amount < 0.0)
        throw new DataSetException("Negative in ");
      else
        sum = sum + amount;
    }
```
56

```
      outFile.println( "Average for " + dataSetName
                     + " is " + sum/12.0 );
    }
    catch (IOException except)
    {
      outFile.println("IOException with site "
                    + dataSetName);
      System.exit(0);
    }
    catch (NumberFormatException except)
    {
      outFile.println("NumberFormatException in site "
                    + dataSetName);
    }
    catch (DataSetException except)
    {
      outFile.println(except.getMessage( ) + dataSetName);
    }
  }
}
```
57

**Notes**

## Notes

```
public static void main( String[ ] args )
            throws FileNotFoundException, IOException
{
    String      dataSetName;        // Reporting station name
    BufferedReader  inFile;         // Data file
    PrintWriter outFile;            // Output file

    inFile = new BufferedReader(
                    new FileReader("rainData.dat"));

    outFile = new PrintWriter(
                    new FileWriter("outfile.dat"));

                // Get name of reporting station
    dataSetName = inFile.readLine( );
```

## Rainfall Application

```
    // Processing Loop
    do
    {
       processOneSite(inFile, outFile, dataSetName);
       dataSetName = infile.readLine( );
    } while (dataSetName != null);
    inFile.close( );
    outLine.close( );
    System.exit(0);
}
}
```

# Chapter 11: One-Dimensional Arrays

## Introduction to Java and Software Design

Dale • Weems • Headington

Chapter 11

One-Dimensional Arrays

## Chapter 11 Topics

- Atomic and composite data types
- Declaring and instantiating an array
- The length of an array
- Manipulating the elements in an array
- Using an array to count frequencies
- Passing an array to a method

## Java Primitive Data Types

```
                    primitive
           ┌───────────┼───────────┐
       integral     boolean   floating point
    ┌───┬───┬───┬───┐           ┌─────┬─────┐
   byte char short int long    float    double
```

**Notes**

## Java Data Types

```
              Java Data Types
              /            \
         primitive        reference
        /    |    \       /   |    \
  integral boolean floating array interface class
  /  |  |  |  \     point
byte char short int long  /    \
                      float  double
```

## Scalar Data Type

A scalar data type is a type in which

- the values are ordered and each value is atomic (indivisible)
- `int`, `float`, `double`, and `char` data types are scalar.

## Declare variables to store and total 3 blood pressures

```
int  bp0,  bp1,  bp2;
int  total;
```

bp0   bp1   bp2

```
total =  bp0 + bp1 + bp2;
```

The Student Lecture Companion

## Composite Data Type

A composite data type is a type that

- allows a collection of values to be associated with an identifier of that type.

- In Java, composite types are either classes, interfaces, or arrays.

- There are 2 forms of composite types: unstructured and structured.

## Structured Data Type

A structured data type is a type which

- is an organized collection of components; and allows individual components to be stored and retrieved.

- The organization determines the method used to access individual components.

- An array is a structured data type whose components are accessed by position.

## What if you wanted to store and total 1000 blood pressures?

```
int[ ] bp = new int[1000];
    // declares and instantiates (creates)
    // an array of 1000 int values
    // and initializes all 1000 elements to zero
```

| 0 | 0 | 0 | . . . . | 0 |

bp[0]   bp[1]   bp[2]   . . . .   bp[999]

# Notes

## Arrays

Arrays are data structures consisting of related data items all of the same type.

- An array type is a reference type. Contiguous memory locations are allocated for the array, beginning at the base address of the array.

- A particular element in the array is accessed by using the array name together with the position of the desired element in square brackets. The position is called the index or subscript.

```
double[ ] salesAmt;
salesAmt = new double[6];
```

salesAmt

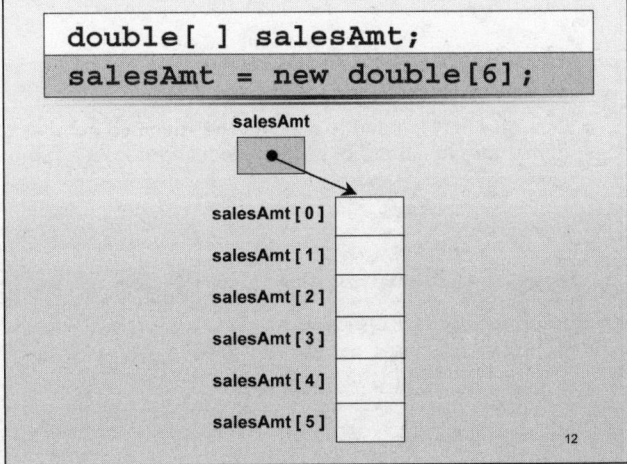

```
double[ ] salesAmt;
salesAmt = new double[6];
```

salesAmt

salesAmt [ 0 ]
salesAmt [ 1 ]
salesAmt [ 2 ]
salesAmt [ 3 ]
salesAmt [ 4 ]
salesAmt [ 5 ]

## Array Definition

An array is a collection of elements, all of the same data type, given a single name.

The subscript (or index) must have an integral value. In Java, the first array element always has subscript 0. The second array element has subscript 1, etc.

When allocated, the elements are automatically initialized to 0 for numeric primitive data type values, to `false` for `boolean` variables, or to `null` for references (non-primitive type values).

## Another Example

- Declare and instantiate an array called `temps` to hold 5 individual double values.

number of elements in the array

```
double[ ] temps = new double[ 5 ] ;
        // declares and allocates memory
```

| 0.0 | 0.0 | 0.0 | 0.0 | 0.0 |
|---|---|---|---|---|
| temps[0] | temps[1] | temps[2] | temps[3] | temps[4] |

indexes or subscripts

## Declaring and Allocating an Array

- Operator `new` is used to allocate the specified number of memory locations of the size needed for DataType.

**SYNTAX FORMS**

```
DataType[ ] ArrayName ;                            // declares array
ArrayName = new DataType [ IntExpression ] ;       // allocates array
```

```
DataType[ ] ArrayName = new DataType [ IntExpression ] ;
```

**Notes**

## Assigning values to individual array elements

```
double[ ]  temps = new double[ 5 ];      // creates array
int     m = 4 ;
temps[ 2 ] = 98.6 ;
temps[ 3 ] = 101.2 ;
temps[ 0 ] = 99.4 ;
temps[ m ] = temps[ 3 ] / 2.0 ;
temps[ 1 ] = temps[ 3 ] - 1.2 ;     // what value is assigned?
```

| 99.4 | ? | 98.6 | 101.2 | 50.6 |
|---|---|---|---|---|
| temps[0] | temps[1] | temps[2] | temps[3] | temps[4] |

## What values are assigned?

```
double[ ]  temps = new double[ 5 ];     // allocates array
int    m ;

for ( m = 0;  m < temps.length ; m++ )
    temps[ m ] = 100.0 + m * 0.2  ;
```

| ? | ? | ? | ? | ? |
|---|---|---|---|---|
| temps[0] | temps[1] | temps[2] | temps[3] | temps[4] |

## Now what values are printed?

```
final  int  ARRAY_SIZE = 5 ;         // named constant
double[ ]  temps;
temps = new double[ ARRAY_SIZE ] ;
int   m ;
.....
for ( m = temps.length-1 ;  m >= 0  ;  m-- )
    System.out.println( "temps[ " + m + " ] = " + temps[ m ] ) ;
```

| 100.0 | 100.2 | 100.4 | 100.6 | 100.8 |
|---|---|---|---|---|
| temps[0] | temps[1] | temps[2] | temps[3] | temps[4] |

The Student Lecture Companion

## Variable subscripts

```
double[ ] temps = new double[ 5 ];
int    m = 3 ;
......
```

What is temps[ m + 1 ] ?

What is temps[ m ] + 1 ?

| 100.0 | 100.2 | 100.4 | 100.6 | 100.8 |
|-------|-------|-------|-------|-------|
| temps[0] | temps[1] | temps[2] | temps[3] | temps[4] |

## Using an initializer list in a declaration

```
int[ ] ages  =  { 40, 13, 20, 19, 36 } ;

for ( int i = 0; i < ages.length ; i++ )
   System.out.println( "ages[ " + i + " ] = " + ages[ i ] ) ;
```

| 40 | 13 | 20 | 19 | 36 |
|----|----|----|----|----|
| ages[0] | ages[1] | ages[2] | ages[3] | ages[4] |

## Passing Arrays as Arguments

- In Java an array is a reference type. What is passed to a method with an array parameter is the address of where the array object is stored.

- The name of the array is actually a reference to an object that contains the array elements and the public instance variable `length`.

## Passing an Array as Parameter

```
public static double average ( int[ ] grades )
// Determines and returns the average grade in an array
{
    int total = 0 ;

    for ( int i = 0 ; i < grades.length ; i++ )
        total = total + grades[ i ] ;

    return (double) total / (double) grades.length ; ;

}
```

## Memory allocated for array

```
int [ ] temps = new int [ 31 ];     // array holds 31 temperatures
```

| 50 | 65 | 70 | 62 | 68 | . . . . . . | | |

temp[0]  temp[1]  temp[2]  temp[3]  temp[4]     . . . . .              temp[30]

## Parallel arrays

### DEFINITION

**Parallel arrays** are 2 or more arrays that have the same index range, and whose elements contain related information, possibly of different data types.

### EXAMPLE

```
final int SIZE = 50;
int[ ] idNumber = new int [SIZE];
float[ ] hourlyWage = new float [SIZE];
```

```
final int SIZE = 50;
int[] idNumber = new int[SIZE];        // parallel arrays hold
float[] hourlyWage = new float[SIZE];  // related information
```

| idNumber | | hourlyWage | |
|---|---|---|---|
| idNumber[0] | 4562 | hourlyWage[0] | 9.68 |
| idNumber[1] | 1235 | hourlyWage[1] | 45.75 |
| idNumber[2] | 6278 | hourlyWage[2] | 12.71 |
| . | . | . | . |
| idNumber[48] | 8754 | hourlyWage[48] | 67.96 |
| idNumber[49] | 2460 | hourlyWage[49] | 8.97 |

## Using arrays for counters

- Write a program to count the number of each alphabet letter in a text file.

| letter | ASCII |
|---|---|
| 'A' | 65 |
| 'B' | 66 |
| 'C' | 67 |
| 'D' | 68 |
| . | . |
| . | . |
| 'Z' | 90 |

**datafile.dat**

This is my text file. It contains many things!
5 + 8 is not 14.
Is it?

```
int[ ] letterCount = new int[26];
```

| | | |
|---|---|---|
| letterCount[0] | 2 | counts 'A' and 'a' |
| letterCount[1] | 0 | counts 'B' and 'b' |
| . | . | . |
| letterCount[24] | 1 | counts 'Y' and 'y' |
| letterCount[25] | 0 | counts 'Z' and 'z' |

**Notes**

## Pseudocode for counting letters

Instantiate dataFile
Read one letter from dataFile
While not EOF dataFile
    If letter is alphabetic character
        Convert uppercase of letter to to index
        Increment letterCount[index] by 1
    Read letter from dataFile
Print characters and frequencies to outFile

## Counting Frequency of Alphabetic Characters

```
int letter ;
. . .                              // read file one character at a time
letter = dataFile.read( );         // priming read
while ( letter != -1 )             // while last read was successful
{
    if ( ( (char) letter >= 'A'  && (char) letter <= 'Z' ) ||
         ( (char) letter >= 'a'  && (char) letter <= 'z' ) )
    {
        index = (int) Character.toUpperCase( (char) letter ) - (int) 'A' ;
        letterCount [ index ] = letterCount [ index ] + 1 ;
    }
    letter = dataFile.read( );     // get next character
}
```

## Printing Frequency of Alphabetic Characters

```
          // print each alphabet letter and its frequency count

for ( index = 0 ; index < letterCount.length ; index ++ )
{
    outFile.println("The total number of "
                    + (char) ( index + (int) 'A' )
                    + letterCount[index]);
}
```

## More about array index

- Array index can be an integral expression of type `char`, `short`, `byte`, or `int`.

- It is programmer's responsibility to make sure that an array index does not go out of bounds. **The index must be within the range 0 through the array's length minus 1.**

- Using an index value outside this range throws an `ArrayIndexOutOfBoundsException`. Prevent this error by using public instance method length.

```
String[ ] groceryItems = new String[10];
```

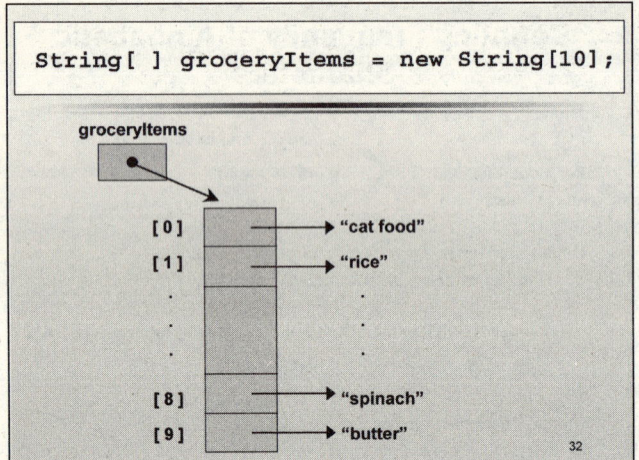

```
String[ ] groceryItems = new String[10];
```

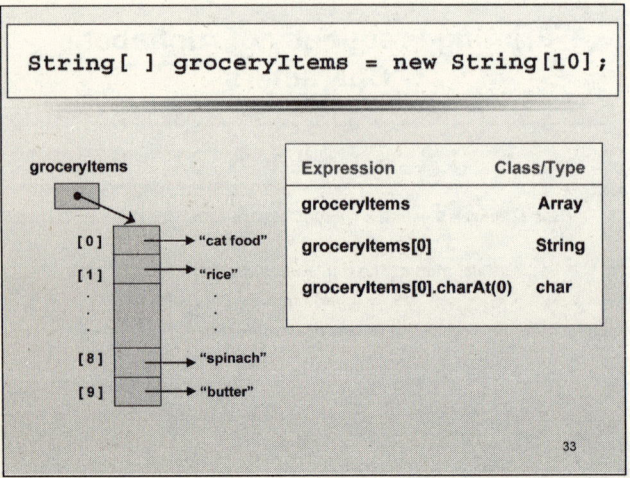

# Notes

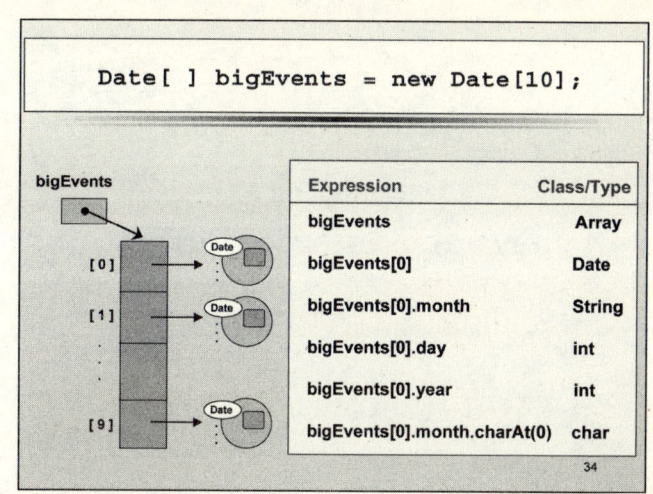

# Chapter 12: Array-Based Lists

## Introduction to Java and Software Design

Dale • Weems • Headington

Chapter 12

Array-Based Lists

## Chapter 12 Topics

- Insertion and Deletion of List Items
- Straight Selection Sort of List Items
- Insertion and Deletion using a Sorted List
- Sequential Search for a List Item
- Binary Search in a Sorted List
- Order of Magnitude of a Function
- Complexity of Searching and Sorting
- Declaring and Using C Strings
- Using the Java `Comparable` Interface

## What is a List?

- A list is a homogeneous collection of elements, with a linear relationship between elements.

- Linear means each list element (except the first) has a unique predecessor, and each element (except the last) has a unique successor.

**Notes**

## Basic Kinds of Class Operations

- **Constructor** -- creates a new instance (object) of a class.
- **Transformer** -- changes the internal state of an object.
- **Observer** -- allows us to observe the state of an object without changing it.

## Additional Class Operations

- **Iterator** -- allows us to process (one by one) all the components in an object).
- **Copy Constructor** -- creates a new instance of a class by copying an existing instance, (possibly altering some or all of its state in the process).

## `class List` Operations

**Transformers**
- insert
- delete

← change state

**Observers**
- isEmpty
- isFull
- length
- isThere

← observe state

**Iterators**
- resetList
- getNextItem

← process components

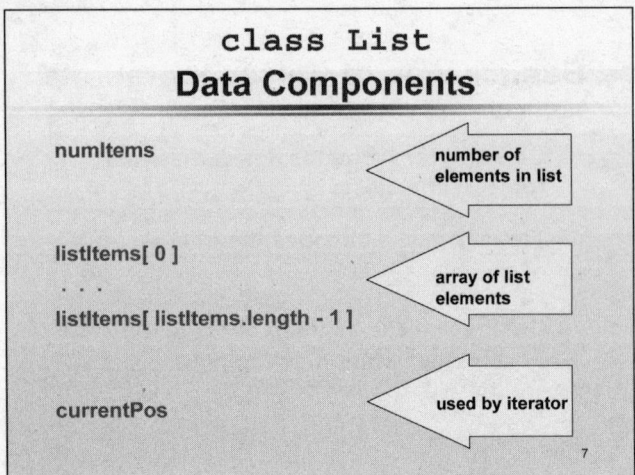
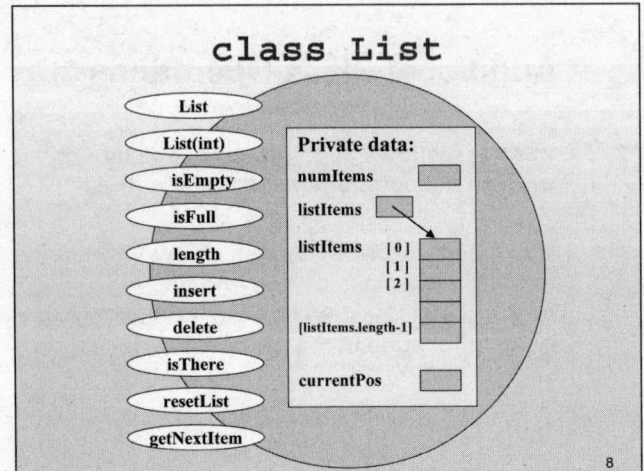
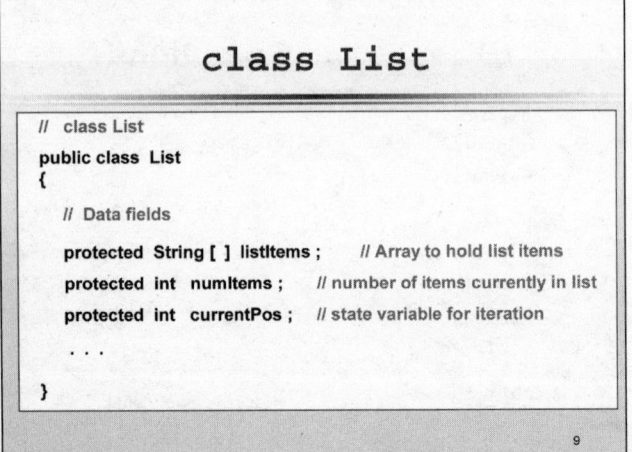

# Notes

## Unsorted and Sorted Lists

| UNSORTED LIST | SORTED LIST |
|---|---|
| Elements are placed into the list in no particular order with respect to their content. | List elements are in an order that is sorted by the content of their keys -- either numerically or alphabetically. |

```
public  List ( )                          // Default Constructor
// Result:  An empty list object has been instantiated with room
// for 100 items
{
    numItems = 0 ;
    listItems = new  String [ 100 ] ;
    currentPos = 0 ;
}
public  List ( int  maxItems )            // Constructor
// Result:  An empty list object has been instantiated with room
// for maxItems items
{
    numItems = 0 ;
    listItems = new  String [ maxItems ] ;
    currentPos = 0 ;
}
```

```
public  boolean  isFull ( )
// Returns true if no room to add a component;  false otherwise
{
    return ( numItems == listItems.length ) ;
}

public  boolean  isEmpty ( )
// Returns true if no components in the list;  false otherwise
{
    return ( numItems == 0 ) ;
}

public  int  length ( )
// Returns the number of components in the list
{
    return  numItems ;
}
```

## List Method insert

```
public void insert ( String item )
// Result: If the list is not full, puts item in the last position in
// the list; otherwise list is unchanged.
{
   if ( !this.isFull( ) )
   {
       listItems [ numItems ] = item ;
       numItems++ ;
   }
}
```

## Before Inserting 64 into an Unsorted List

| numItems | 3 |
|---|---|
| listItems [ 0 ] | 15 |
| [ 1 ] | 39 |
| [ 2 ] | -90 |
| [ 3 ] | |
| . | |
| . | |
| . | |
| [ listItems.length-1 ] | |

item  64

The item will be placed into the numItems location, and numItems will be incremented.

## After Inserting 64 into an Unsorted List

| numItems | 4 |
|---|---|
| listItems [ 0 ] | 15 |
| [ 1 ] | 39 |
| [ 2 ] | -90 |
| [ 3 ] | 64 |
| . | |
| . | |
| . | |
| [ listItems.length-1 ] | |

item  64

The item will be placed into the numItems location, and numItems will be incremented.

**Notes**

## String method `compareTo`

- When comparing objects with ==, the result is only true if both references refer to the exact same object in memory.

- String method `compareTo` uses dictionary type comparison of strings and returns 0 if they have the exact same letters in the exact same order. It returns a negative number if the invoking String is less than the String passed as a parameter; and returns a positive number if the invoking String is greater than the String that is passed.

## Values of each expression

```
String  s1 = new  String( "today" );
String  s2 = new  String( "yesterday" );
String  s3 = new  String( "today" );
String  s4 = new  String ( "Today" );
```

```
s1.compareTo(s2)                -5
s1 == s3                        false
s1.compareTo(s3)                0
s1.compareTo(s4)                32
```

## List Method `isThere`

```
public boolean   isThere ( String item )
// Returns true if item is in the list; false otherwise

{   int   index = 0 ;

    while  ( index < numItems
              && listItems[ index ].compareTo(item) != 0 )
        index++ ;

    return  ( index < numItems ) ;
}
```

## delete algorithm for `class List`

- Find the position of the element to be deleted from the list.
- Eliminate the item being deleted by *shifting up* all the following list elements.
- Decrement numItems.

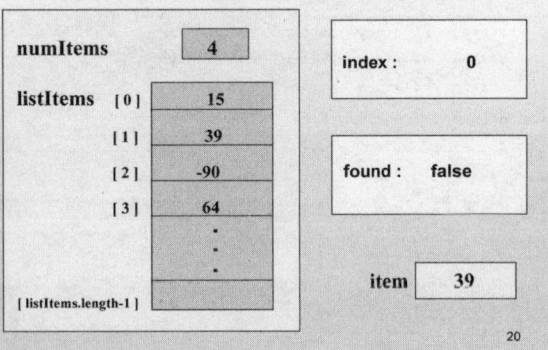

### Deleting 39 from a List

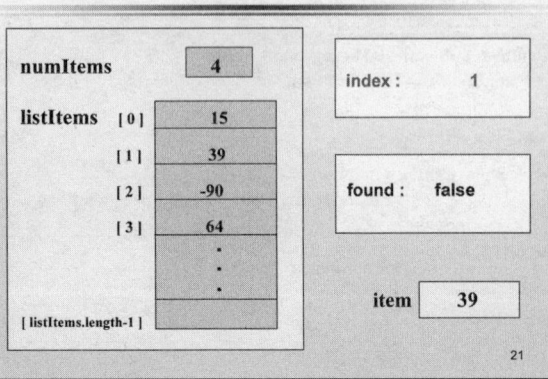

### Deleting 39 from a List

**Notes**

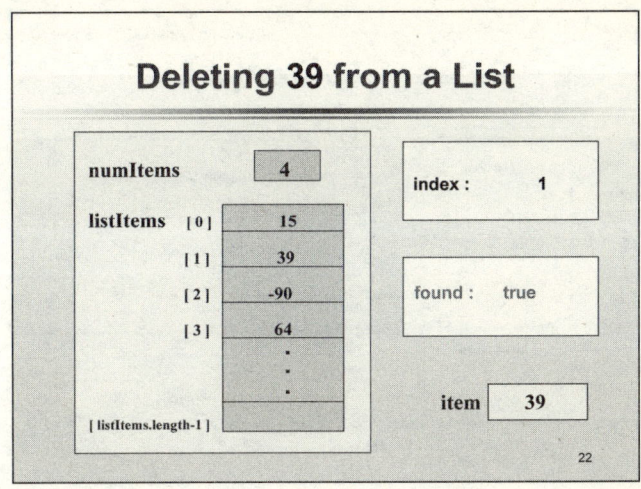

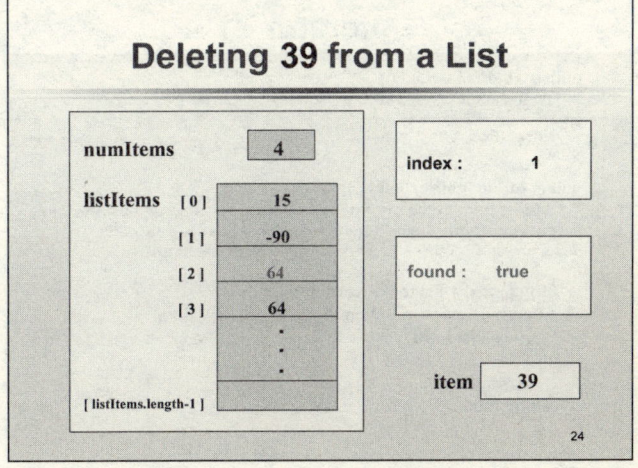

## Deleting 39 from a List

numItems: 3

listItems:
- [0] 15
- [1] -90
- [2] 64
- [3] 64
- .
- .
- .
- [listItems.length-1]

index: 1

found: true

item: 39

---

```java
public void delete ( String item )
// Result: Removes item from the list if it is there; otherwise
// list is unchanged.
{
    int index = 0 ;
    boolean found = false ;
    while ( index < numItems  && !found )
    {
        if ( listItems[index].compareTo( item ) == 0 )
            found = true;
        else
            index++;
    }
    // if item found, shift remainder of list up to delete item
    if ( found )
    {
        for ( int count = index ; count < numItems - 1; count++ )
            listItems [ count ] = listItems [ count + 1 ] ;
        numItems-- ;
    }
}
```

## Iterator

```java
public void  resetList ( )
// The iteration is initialized by setting currentPos to 0
{
    currentPos = 0;
}
public String  getNextItem ( )
// Returns item at the curentPos positon;  increments currentPos;
// resets currentPos to first item after last item is returned.
// Assumes:  no transformers invoked since last call.
{
    String next = listItems[ currentPos ] ;
    if ( currentPos == numItems - 1 )
        currentPos = 0 ;
    else
        currentPos++;
    return next ;
}
```

# Notes

### Straight Selection Sort Process

- Examines the entire list to select the smallest element. Then places that element where it belongs (with array index 0).

- Examines the remaining list to select the smallest element from it. Then places that element where it belongs (with array index 1).
  .
  .
  .
- Examines the last 2 remaining list elements to select the smallest one. Then places that element where it belongs in the array.

### Selection Sort Algorithm

FOR passCount going from 0 through numItems - 2
    Find minimum value in listItems [ passCount . . numItems-1 ]
    Swap minimum value with listItems [ passCount ]

numItems = 5

| | | | | |
|---|---|---|---|---|
| listItems [ 0 ] | 40 | | | 25 |
| listItems [ 1 ] | 100 | pass = 0 | | 100 |
| listItems [ 2 ] | 60 | 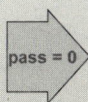 | | 60 |
| listItems [ 3 ] | 25 | | | 40 |
| listItems [ 4 ] | 80 | | | 80 |

```
public void  selectSort ( )
// Arranges list into ascending order using straight selection sort
{   String      temp ;
    int         passCount ;
    int         sIndex ;
    int         minIndex ;      // index of minimum so far
    for ( passCount = 0 ; passCount < numItems - 1 ; passCount++ )
    {
        minIndex = passCount ;
        // find index of smallest of
        // listItems [ passCount ] . . . listItems[ numItems-1 ]
        for ( sIndex = passCount + 1 ; sIndex < numItems ; sIndex++ )
            if  ( listItems [ sIndex ].compareTo( listItems [ minIndex ] ) < 0 )
                minIndex = sIndex ;
        temp = listItems [ minIndex ] ;         // swap
        listItems [ minIndex ] = listItems [ passCount ] ;
        listItems [ passCount ] = temp ;
    }
}
```

## Unsorted and Sorted Lists

**UNSORTED LIST**
Elements are placed into the list in no particular order with respect to their content.

**SORTED LIST**
List elements are in an order that is sorted by the content of their keys -- either numerically or alphabetically.

## class SortedList

- SortedList
- SortedList(int)
- isEmpty
- isFull
- length
- insert
- delete
- isThere
- resetList
- getNextItem

Private data:
- numItems
- listItems
- listItems [0] [1] [2] ... [listItems.length-1]
- currentPos

```
// SPECIFICATION FILE    ARRAY-BASED SORTED LIST    ( slist.h )
   int MAX_LENGTH = 50 ;
typedef  int  ItemType ;

class SortedList
{
public :                  // public member functions

   SortedList ( ) ;                            // constructor
   boolean      isEmpty ( ) ;
   boolean            isFull ( ) ;
   int          length ( )  ;        // returns numItems of list
   void         insert ( ItemType  item ) ;
   void         delete ( ItemType  item ) ;
   boolean      isThere( ItemType  item )  ;
   void         Print ( ) ;

private :            // private data members

   int         numItems ;             // number of values currently stored
   ItemType    listItems[MAX_LENGTH] ;
   void  BinSearch ( ItemType item, boolean  found, int  position )  ;
} ;
```

# Notes

## Changing methods

Which method specifications and implementations must change to ensure that any instance of `class SortedList` remains sorted at all times?

- insert

## insert algorithm for `class SortedList`

- Create space for the new item by *shifting down* all the larger list elements.
- Put the new item in the list.
- Increment numItems.

```
public void   insert ( String  item )
// If the list is not full, puts item in its proper place in the list;
// otherwise list is unchanged.
// Assumption:  item is not already in the list.
{
   if ( !this.isFull( ) )
   {                         //  find proper location for new element
      int  index  =  numItems - 1 ;
                   // starting at bottom of array shift down values
                   // larger than item to make room for new item
      while ( index >= 0  &&
                    item.compareTo( listItems [ index ] ) < 0 )
      {
         listItems [ index + 1 ]  =  listItems [ index ] ;
         index-- ;
      }
      listItems [ index +1] = item ;       // insert item into array
      numItems++ ;
   }
}
```

### List class hierarchy

- List
  - ListWithSort
  - SortedList

### Alternate hierarchy with `abstract class List`

- List
  - UnsortedList
    - ListWithSort
  - SortedList

### Improving method `isThere` for `SortedList`

Recall that with the unsorted class List we examined each list element beginning with `listItems[0]`, until we either found a match with item, or we had examined all the elements in the unsorted List.

How can the searching algorithm be improved for class SortedList?

# Notes

## Searching for 55 in a `SortedList`

| numItems | 4 |
|---|---|
| listItems [0] | 15 |
| [1] | 39 |
| [2] | 64 |
| [3] | 90 |
| . | |
| . | |
| . | |
| [ listItems.length-1 ] | |

A sequential search for 55 can stop when 64 has been examined.

item: 55

## Binary Search in SortedList

- Examines the element in the middle of the array. Is it the sought item? If so, stop searching. Is the middle element too small? Then start looking in second half of array. Is the middle element too large? Then begin looking in first half of the array.

- Repeat the process in the half of the array that should be examined next.

- Stop when item is found, or when there is nowhere else to look and item has not been found.

```java
public boolean isThere ( String item )
// Assumes: List items are in ascending order
// Returns true if item is in the list; false otherwise.
// Uses Binary Search algorithm.
{
    int     first = 0;
    int     last = numItems - 1 ;
    int     middle ;
    boolean found = false ;
    while ( last >= first && !found )
    {   middle = ( first + last ) / 2 ;          // INDEX OF MIDDLE ELEMENT

        if ( item.compareTo( listItems [ middle ] ) == 0 )
            found = true ;                        // ITEM HAS BEEN FOUND
        else if ( item.compareTo( listItems [ middle ] ) < 0 )
            last = middle - 1 ;                   // LOOK IN FIRST HALF NEXT
        else
            first = middle + 1 ;                  // LOOK IN SECOND HALF NEXT
    }
    return found ;
}
```

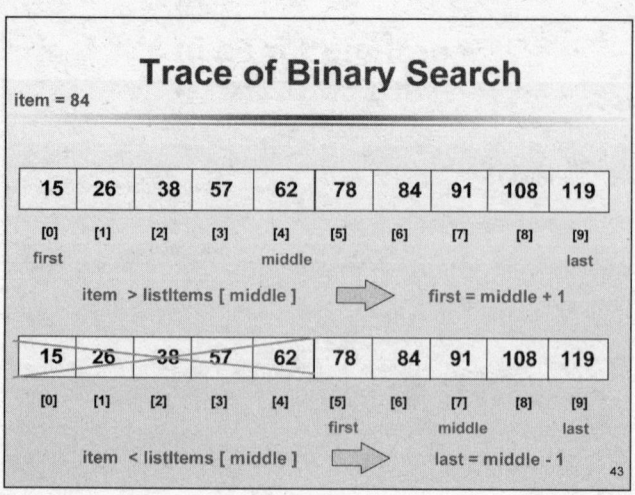

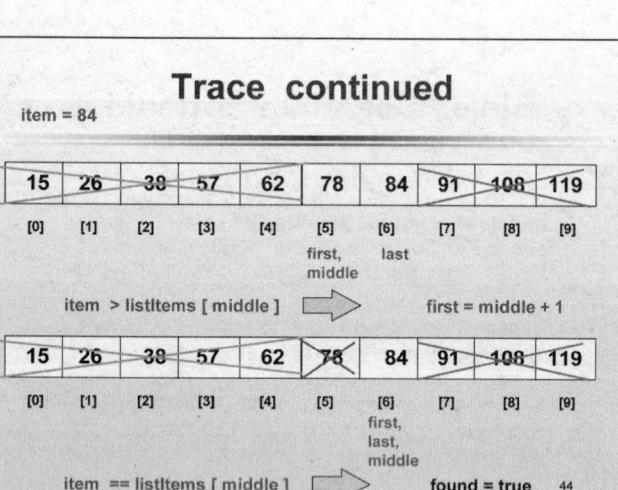

### Another Binary Search Trace

item = 45

| 15 | 26 | 38 | 57 | 62 | 78 | 84 | 91 | 108 | 119 |
|----|----|----|----|----|----|----|----|-----|-----|
|[0]|[1]|[2]|[3]|[4]|[5]|[6]|[7]|[8]|[9]|

first — middle — last

item < listItems [ middle ] ⇒ last = middle - 1

| 15 | 26 | 38 | 57 | 62 | 78 | 84 | 91 | 108 | 119 |
|----|----|----|----|----|----|----|----|-----|-----|
|[0]|[1]|[2]|[3]|[4]|[5]|[6]|[7]|[8]|[9]|

first — middle — last

item > listItems [ middle ] ⇒ first = middle + 1

# Notes

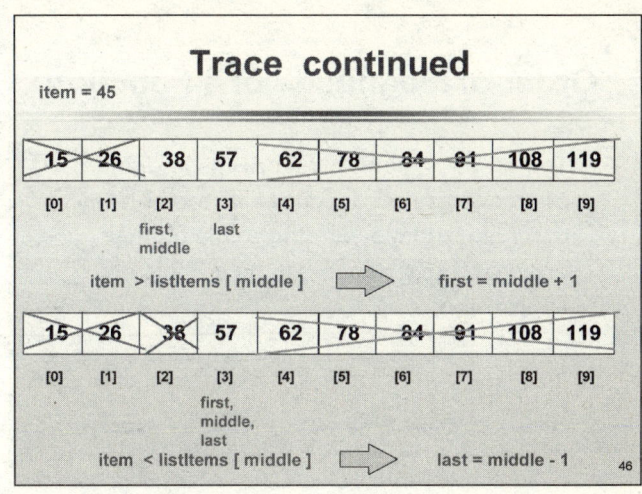

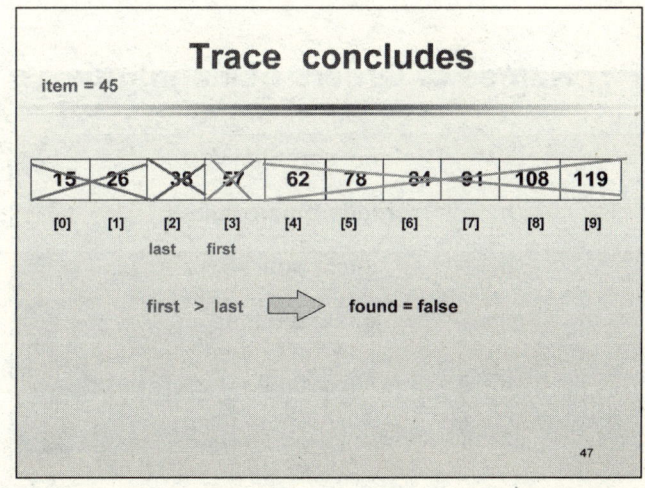

## Order of Magnitude of a Function

The order of magnitude, or Big-O notation, of an expression describes the complexity of an algorithm according to the highest order of N that appears in its complexity expression.

## Names of Orders of Magnitude

| | |
|---|---|
| $O(1)$ | constant time |
| $O(\log_2 N)$ | logarithmic time |
| $O(N)$ | linear time |
| $O(N^2)$ | quadratic time |
| $O(N^3)$ | cubic time |

| N | $\log_2 N$ | $N^2$ |
|---|---|---|
| 1 | 0 | 1 |
| 2 | 1 | 4 |
| 4 | 2 | 16 |
| 8 | 3 | 64 |
| 16 | 4 | 256 |
| 32 | 5 | 1,024 |
| 64 | 6 | 4,096 |
| 1,024 | 10 | 1,048,576 |

**Notes**

## Notes

### Big-O Comparison of List Operations

| OPERATION | UnsortedList | SortedList |
|---|---|---|
| isThere | O(N) | O(N) sequential search<br>O($\log_2 N$) binary search |
| insert | O(1) | O(N) |
| delete | O(N) | O(N) |
| selectSort | O($N^2$) | |

### `Comparable` Interface

- Is part of the standard Java class library.
- Any class that implements the Comparable interface must implement method compareTo.
- String implements the Comparable interface.

# Chapter 13: Multidimensional Arrays and Numeric Computation

---

**Introduction to Java and Software Design**

Dale • Weems • Headington

Chapter 13

Multidimensional Arrays and Numeric Computation

---

**Chapter 13 Topics**

- Declaring and Using a Two-Dimensional Array
- Two-Dimensional Arrays as Parameters
- Returning Two-Dimensional Arrays from Methods
- Ragged Arrays
- Declaring and Using a Multidimensional Array

---

**Java Data Types**

primitive
- integral: byte, char, short, int, long
- boolean
- floating point: float, double

reference
- array, interface, class

**Notes**

**Notes**

## Two-Dimensional Array

**is a** collection of components, all of the same type or class, structured in two dimensions, (referred to as rows and columns). Each component is accessed by a pair of indexes representing the component's position in each dimension.

## Syntax for Array Declaration

**Array Declaration**

```
DataType [ ] [ ] ArrayName;
```

**EXAMPLES**

```
double[][] alpha;
String[][] beta;
int[][] data;
```

## Two-Dimensional Array Instantiation

**Two-Dimensional Array Instantiation**

```
ArrayName = new DataType [Expression1] [Expression2] ;
```

where each Expression has an integral value and specifies the number of components in that dimension.

## Two-Dimensional Array Instantiation

**Two-Dimensional Array Instantiation**

ArrayName = new DataType [Expression1] [Expression2] ;

TWO FORMS FOR DECLARATION AND INSTANTIATION

```
int[][] data;
data = new int[6][12];
```
OR
```
int[][] data = new int[6][12];
```

## Indexes in Two-Dimensional Arrays

**Individual array elements are accessed by a pair of indexes. The first index represents the element's row, and the second index represents the element's column.**

```
int[ ][ ] data;
data = new int[6][12] ;

data[2][7] = 4 ;        // row 2, column 7
```

## Accessing an Individual Component

```
int [ ][ ] data;
data = new int [ 6 ][ 12 ] ;
data [ 2 ][ 7 ] = 4 ;
```

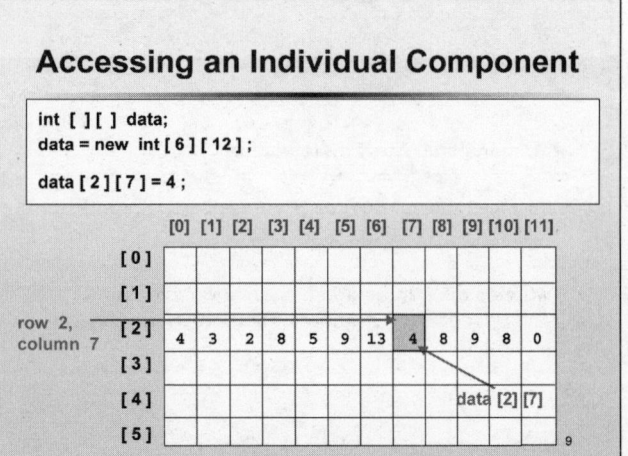

# Notes

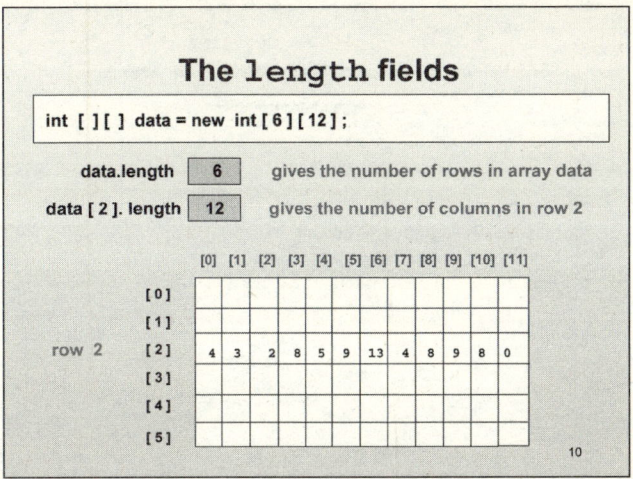

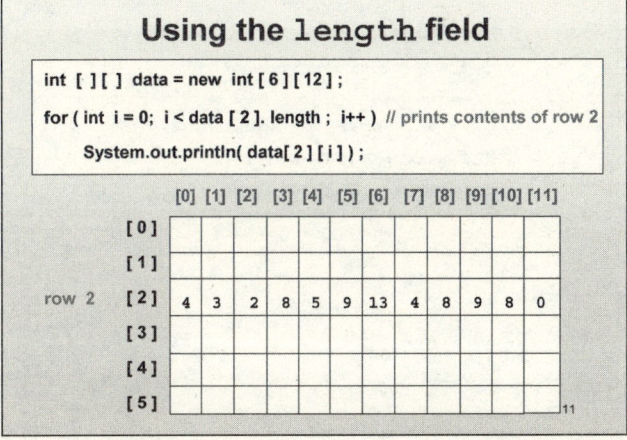

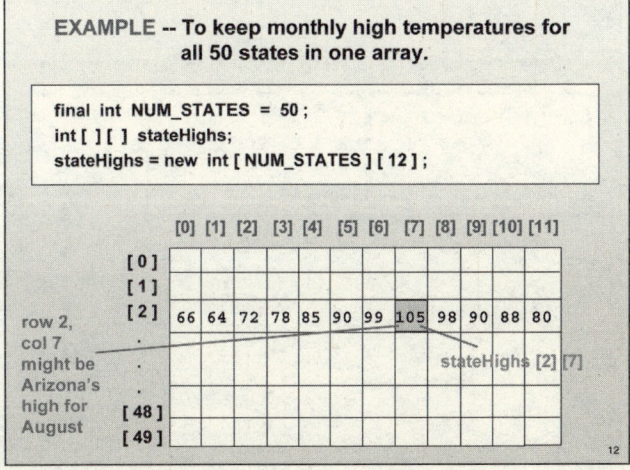

### Finding the average high temperature for Arizona

```
int  total  = 0 ;
int  month ;
int  average ;
for ( month = 0 ; month < 12 ; month ++ )
    total = total + stateHighs [ 2 ] [ month ] ;
average = ( int ) ( ( double) total / 12.0  + 0.5 ) ;
```

average
**85**

---

## Two-Dimensional Array

**In Java, actually, a two-dimensional array is itself a one-dimensional array of references to one-dimensional arrays.**

---

## Using Initializer Lists

```
int [ ] [ ] hits = { { 2, 1, 0, 3, 2 },
                     { 1, 1, 2, 3, 4 },
                     { 1, 0, 0, 0, 0 },
                     { 0, 1, 2, 1, 1 } };
```

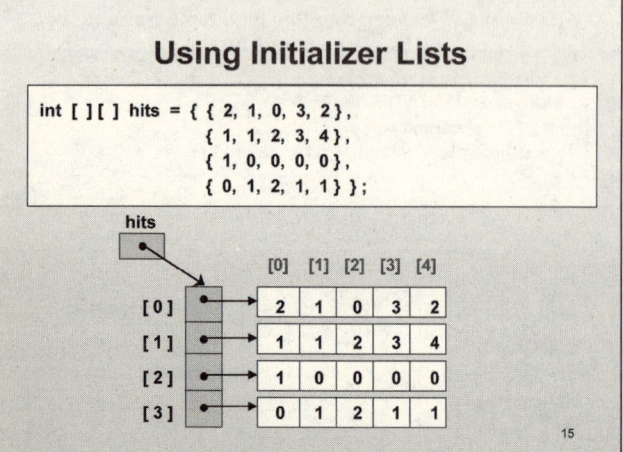

# Notes

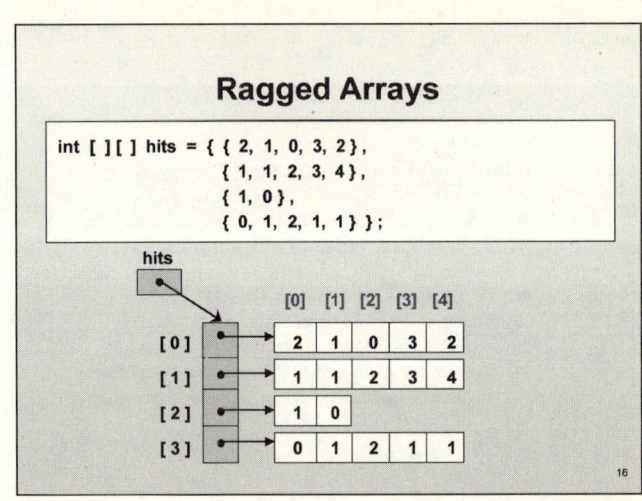

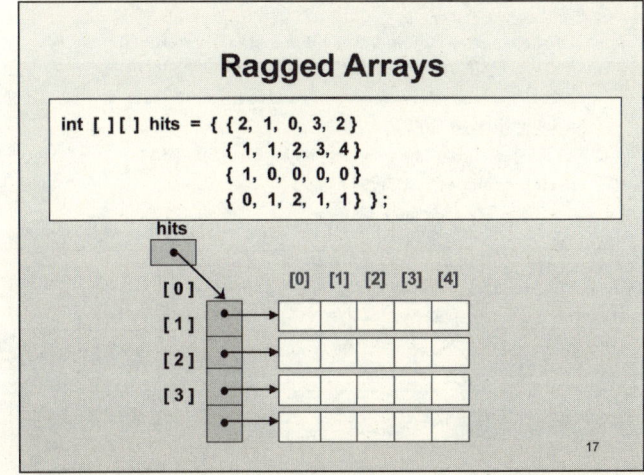

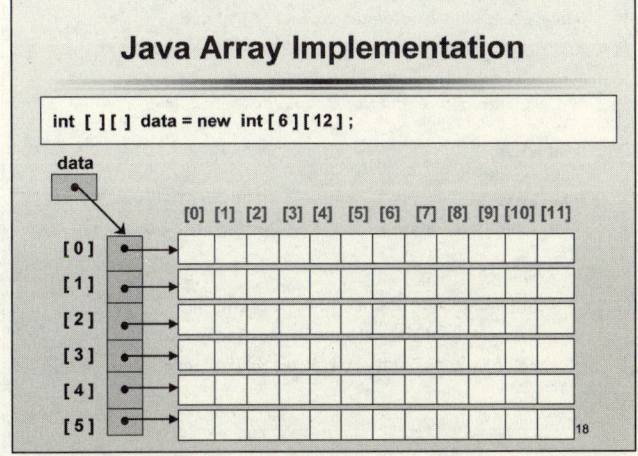

## Arrays as parameters

- Just as with a one-dimensional array, when a two- (or higher) dimensional array is passed as an argument, the base address of the caller's array is sent to the method.

- Because Java has a `length` field associated with each array that contains the number of slots defined for the array, we do not have to pass this information as an additional parameter.

---

Write a method using the two-dimensional stateHighs array to fill a one-dimensional stateAverages array

```
final int NUM_STATES = 50 ;
int [ ] [ ]  stateHighs = new  int [ NUM_STATES ] [ 12 ] ;
int  stateAverages [ NUM_STATES ] ;
```

|         |    |      | [0] | [1] | [2] | [3] | [4] | [5] | [6] | [7] | [8] | [9] | [10] | [11] |
|---------|----|------|-----|-----|-----|-----|-----|-----|-----|-----|-----|-----|------|------|
|         |    | [0]  |     |     |     |     |     |     |     |     |     |     |      |      |
| Alaska  | 62 | [1]  | 43  | 42  | 50  | 55  | 60  | 78  | 80  | 85  | 81  | 72  | 63   | 40   |
| Arizona | 85 | [2]  | 66  | 64  | 72  | 78  | 85  | 90  | 99  | 105 | 98  | 90  | 88   | 80   |
|         |    | [48] |     |     |     |     |     |     |     |     |     |     |      |      |
|         |    | [49] |     |     |     |     |     |     |     |     |     |     |      |      |

---

```java
public static void  findAverages(  int [ ] [ ]  stateHighs,
                                   int [ ]  stateAverages )
// Result:  stateAverages[ 0..NUM_STATES] contains rounded
//          average high temperature for each state
{
   int state;
   int month;
   int total;
   for ( state = 0 ; state < stateAverages.length ; state++ )
   {
      total = 0 ;
      for ( month = 0 ; month < 12 ; month++ )
         total = total + stateHighs [ state ] [ month ] ;
      stateAverages [ state ] = ( int ) ( ( double) total / 12.0  + 0.5 ) ;
   }
}
```

**Notes**

## Declaring Multidimensional Arrays

**EXAMPLE OF THREE-DIMENSIONAL ARRAY**

final int NUM_DEPTS = 5;   // mens, womens, childrens, electronics, furniture

final int NUM_STORES = 3;   // White Marsh, Owings Mills, Towson

int [ ] [ ] [ ]  monthlySales;

monthlySales = new int [ NUM_DEPTS ] [ 12 ] [ NUM_STORES ];

                                       rows     columns     sheets

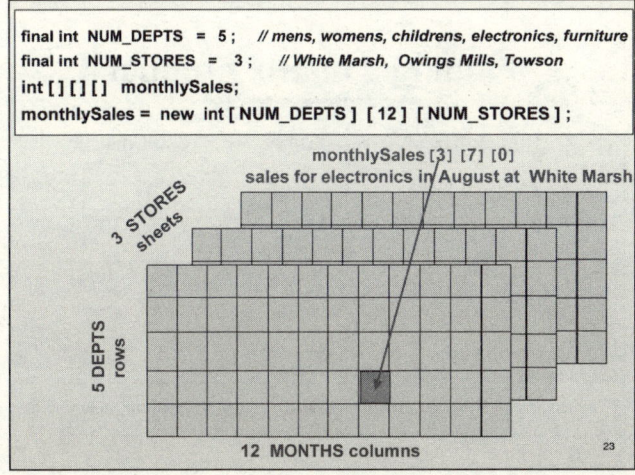

final int NUM_DEPTS = 5;   // mens, womens, childrens, electronics, furniture
final int NUM_STORES = 3;   // White Marsh, Owings Mills, Towson
int [ ] [ ] [ ]  monthlySales;
monthlySales = new int [ NUM_DEPTS ] [ 12 ] [ NUM_STORES ];

monthlySales [3] [7] [0]
sales for electronics in August at White Marsh

3 STORES sheets
5 DEPTS rows
12 MONTHS columns

## Adding a fourth dimension . . .

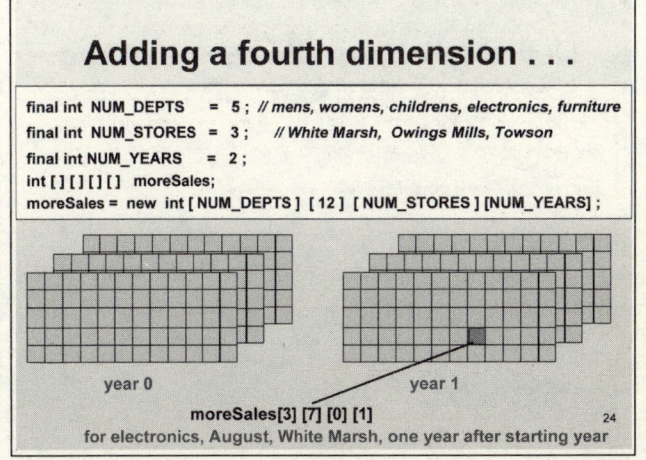

final int NUM_DEPTS = 5;   // mens, womens, childrens, electronics, furniture
final int NUM_STORES = 3;   // White Marsh, Owings Mills, Towson
final int NUM_YEARS = 2;
int [ ] [ ] [ ] [ ]  moreSales;
moreSales = new int [ NUM_DEPTS ] [ 12 ] [ NUM_STORES ] [NUM_YEARS];

year 0      year 1

**moreSales[3] [7] [0] [1]**
for electronics, August, White Marsh, one year after starting year

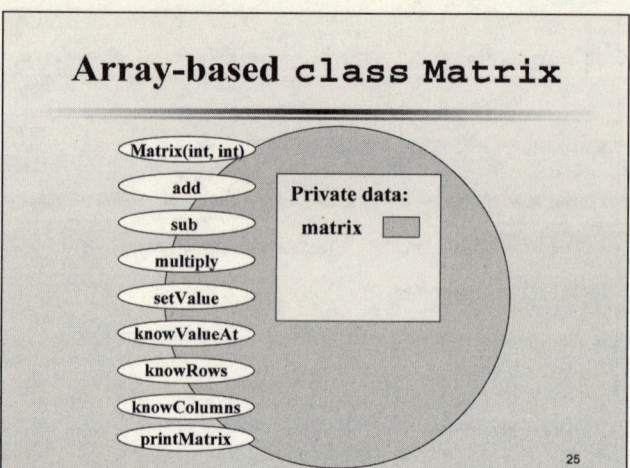

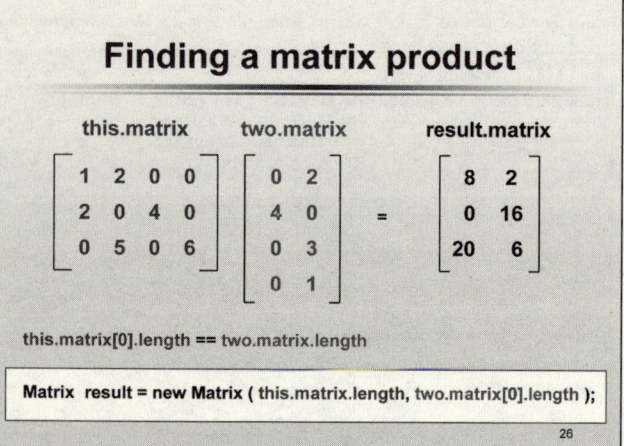

### Defining class MatException

```
// Defines an Exception class for signaling Matrix errors
package  matrix;

public class MatException extends Exception
{
  public MatException( )
  {
    super( );
  }

  public MatException( String message )
  {
    super( message );
  }
}
```

# Notes

```java
// This class allows matrix operations.

package matrix;
import java.io.*;
public class Matrix
{
   // Private data field
   private double[][]  matrix;

   public Matrix (int rows, int columns)
   // Create empty matrix
   {
       matrix = new double[rows][columns];
   }

   public double knowValueAt (int row, int col)
   // Returns value at matrix[row][col]
   {
       return  matrix[row][col];
   }
```

```java
// Matrix class continued

   public int knowRows ( )
   // Returns the number of rows in matrix
   {
       return  matrix.length;
   }

   public int knowColumns ( )
   // Returns the number of columns in matrix
   {
       return  matrix[0].length;
   }

   public void setValue (double dataItem, int row, int col)
   // Result:  matrix[row][col] has been set to dataItem
   {
       matrix[row][col] = dataItem;
   }
```

## Method `printMatrix`

```java
// Matrix class continued

   public void printMatrix (PrintWriter outFile)
   // Result:  matrix is written to OutFile by row
   {
      for (int row = 0; row < matrix.length; row++)
      {
         for (int col = 0; col < matrix[0].length; col++)
            outFile.print(matrix[row][col] + "  ");
         outFile.println( );
      }
   }
```

```java
public Matrix add (Matrix two)   throws MatException
// Returns the sum of this and two. Throws MatException
// if the matrices cannot be added or overflow occurs.
{
   if (matrix.length != two.matrix.length ||
              matrix[0].length != two.matrix[0].length)
      throw new
        MatException(new String("Illegal matrix addition."));
   else
   {
      Matrix result = new Matrix(matrix.length,
                             matrix[0].length);
      for (int row = 0; row < matrix.length; row++)
         for (int col = 0; col < matrix[0].length; col++)
         {
            result.matrix[row][col] = matrix[row][col]
                               + two.matrix[row][col];
            if (Double.isInfinite(result.matrix[row][col]))
               throw new
                 MatException(new String("Addition overflow");
         }
      return result;
   }
}
```
31

```java
public Matrix sub (Matrix two)   throws MatException
// Returns two subtracted from this. Throws MatException
// if the matrices cannot be subtracted or overflow occurs.
{
   if (matrix.length != two.matrix.length ||
              matrix[0].length != two.matrix[0].length)
      throw new
        MatException(new String("Illegal matrix subtract."));
   else
   {
      Matrix result = new Matrix(matrix.length,
                             matrix[0].length);
      for (int row = 0; row < matrix.length; row++)
         for (int col = 0; col < matrix[0].length; col++)
         {
            result.matrix[row][col] = matrix[row][col]
                               - two.matrix[row][col];
            if (Double.isInfinite(result.matrix[row][col]))
               throw new
                 MatException(new String("Subtract overflow"));
         }
      return result;
   }
}
```
32

```java
public Matrix multiply (Matrix two)   throws MatException
// Returns this times two. Throws MatException
// if the matrices cannot be multiplied or overflow occurs.
{
   if (matrix.length != two.matrix.length ||
              matrix[0].length != two.matrix[0].length)
      throw new
        MatException(new String("Illegal matrix addition."));
   else
   {
      Matrix result = new Matrix(matrix.length,
                             two.matrix[0].length);
      for (int row = 0; row < matrix.length; row++)
         for (int col = 0; col < matrix[0].length; col++)
         {
            result.matrix[row][col] =
                        dotProduct(row, col, two);
            if (Double.isInfinite(result.matrix[row][col]))
               throw new
                 MatException(new String("Multiply overflow"));
         }
      return result;
   }
}
```
33

**Notes**

## Notes

### End of class Matrix

```
// Helper method
private double dotProduct(int row, int col, Matrix two)
// Returns the dot product of row of this and column of two
{
    double total = 0;
    for (int index = 0; index < two.matrix.length; index++)
        total = total + matrix[row][index] *
                        two.matrix[index][col];
    return total;

}
}
```

# Chapter 14: Recursion

## Introduction to Java and Software Design

Dale • Weems • Headington

Chapter 14

Recursion

## Chapter 14 Topics

- Meaning of Recursion
- Base Case and General Case in Recursive Definitions
- Writing Recursive Algorithms with Simple Variables
- Writing Recursive Algorithms with Structured Variables
- Understanding How Recursion Works

## Recursive Call

- A **recursive call** is a method call in which the method being called is the same as the one making the call.
- In other words, *recursion occurs when a method calls itself!*
- But we need to avoid making an infinite sequence of method calls (infinite recursion).

## Finding a Recursive Solution

- A recursive solution to a problem must be written carefully.
- The idea is for each successive recursive call to bring you one step closer to a situation in which the problem can easily be solved.
- This easily solved situation is called the base case.
- Each recursive algorithm must have at least one base case, as well as a general (recursive) case.

## General format for many recursive methods

```
if  (some easily-solved condition)     // Base case

    solution statement

else                                   // General case

    recursive method call
```

SOME EXAMPLES . . .

## Writing a recursive method to find the sum of the numbers from 1 to n

**DISCUSSION**

The method call summation(4) should have value 10, because that is 1 + 2 + 3 + 4 .

For an easily-solved situation, the sum of the numbers from 1 to 1 is certainly just 1.

So our base case could be along the lines of

```
if ( n == 1 )
    return 1;
```

## Writing a recursive method to find the sum of the numbers from 1 to n

Now for the general case...

The sum of the numbers from 1 to n, that is,
1 + 2 + . . . + n    can be written as

n  +  the sum of the numbers from 1 to (n - 1),
that is, n + 1 + 2 + . . . + (n - 1)

or,    n  +   summation(n - 1)

And notice that the recursive call  summation(n - 1) gets us "closer" to the base case of  summation(1)

## Finding the sum of the numbers from 1 to n

```
public static int summation ( int  n )
// Returns sum of numbers from 1 to n
// Assumption:  n is greater than 0
// Computes the sum of the numbers from 1 to n by
// adding n to the sum of the numbers from 1 to (n-1)
{
   if  ( n == 1)                          // Base case
       return 1 ;
   else                                   // General case
       return ( n + summation ( n - 1 ) ) ;
}
```

## summation(4) Execution

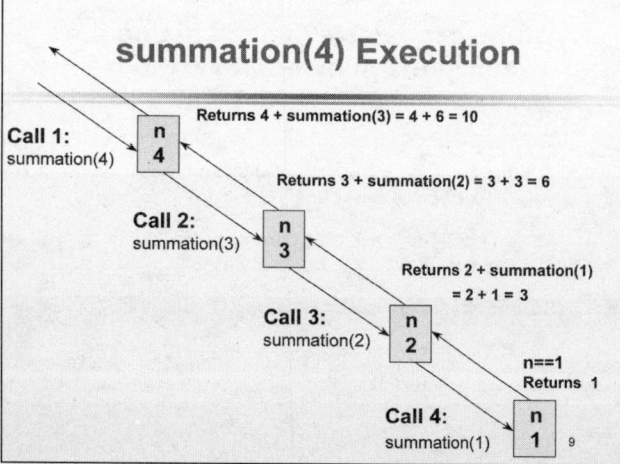

Call 1: summation(4)   n=4   Returns 4 + summation(3) = 4 + 6 = 10

Call 2: summation(3)   n=3   Returns 3 + summation(2) = 3 + 3 = 6

Call 3: summation(2)   n=2   Returns 2 + summation(1) = 2 + 1 = 3

Call 4: summation(1)   n=1   n==1 Returns 1

**Notes**

### Writing a recursive method to find n factorial

**DISCUSSION**

The method call factorial(4) should have value 24, because that is 4 * 3 * 2 * 1.

For a situation in which the answer is known, the value of 0! is 1.

So our base case could be along the lines of

```
if ( number == 0 )
    return 1;
```

### Writing a recursive method to find factorial(n)

Now for the general case . . .

The value of factorial(n) can be written as n * the product of the numbers from (n - 1) to 1, that is,

$$n * \underbrace{(n - 1) * \ldots * 1}$$

or,    n * factorial(n - 1)

And notice that the recursive call factorial(n - 1) gets us "closer" to the base case of factorial(0).

### Recursive Solution

```java
public static int factorial ( int number )
// Assumption: number is greater than or equal to 0.
{
  if ( number == 0)                // Base case
      return 1 ;
  else                             // General case

      return number * factorial ( number - 1 ) ;
}
```

## Another example where recursion comes naturally

- From mathematics, we know that

  $2^0 = 1$  and  $2^5 = 2 * 2^4$

- In general,

  $x^0 = 1$  and  $x^n = x * x^{n-1}$

  for integer x, and integer n > 0.

- Here we are defining $x^n$ recursively, in terms of $x^{n-1}$

---

```
// Recursive definition of power function
public static int power ( int  x,  int  n )
// Assumptions:   n is greater than or equal to 0.
//                x and n are not both zero
// Returns x raised to the power n.
{
    if ( n == 0 )
        return  1;          // Base case
    else                    // General case
        return ( x * power ( x , n-1 ) ) ;
}
```

Of course, an alternative would have been to use looping instead of a recursive call in the method body.

---

## Extending the definition

- What is the value of $2^{-3}$?  Again from mathematics, we know that it is

  $2^{-3} = 1 / 2^3 = 1 / 8$

- In general,

  $x^n = 1 / x^{-n}$

  for non-zero x, and integer n < 0.

- Here we are again defining $x^n$ recursively, in terms of $x^{-n}$ when n < 0.

# Notes

```
// Recursive definition of power function

public static double power ( double x, int n )
// Returns x raised to the power n.
// Assumption:   x is not zero and n has a value.
{
    if ( n == 0 )                    // Base case
        return 1;
    else if ( n > 0 )                // First general case
        return ( x * power ( x , n - 1 ) );
    else                             // Second general case
        return ( 1.0 / power ( x , - n ) );
}
```

## At Times Base Case Can Be: Do Nothing

```
public static void printStars ( int n )
// Assumption:  n is greater than or equal to zero
// Result:   n stars have been printed, one to a line
{
    if ( n <= 0 )                    // Base case
            // Do nothing
    else                             // General case
    {   outFile.println( "*" ) ;
        printStars ( n - 1 ) ;
    }
}
```
// CAN REWRITE AS . . .

## Recursive Void Function

```
public static void printStars ( int n )
// Assumption:  n is greater than or equal to zero
// Result:   n stars have been printed, one to a line
{
    if ( n > 0 )                     // General case
    {   outFile.println( "*" ) ;
        printStars ( n - 1 ) ;
    }
            // Base case is empty else-clause
}
```

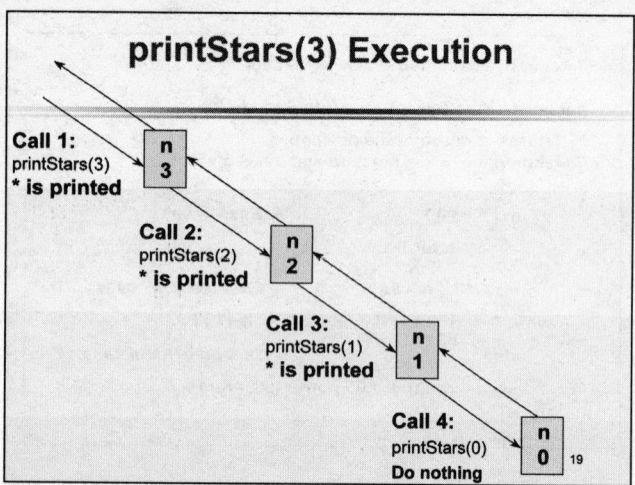

## Recursive Mystery Function

```
public static int find( int b, int a )
// Simulates a familiar integer operator
// Assumption:   a is greater than zero
//               and b is greater than or equal to zero
// Returns  ???
{
   if ( b < a )                          // Base case
      return 0 ;
   else                                  // General case
      return ( 1 + find ( b - a , a ) ) ;
}
```

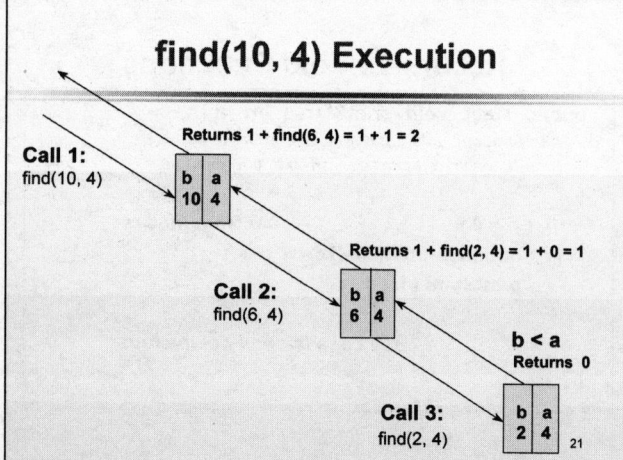

**Notes**

# Notes

## Writing a recursive method to print array elements in reverse order

**DISCUSSION**

For this task, we will use the heading:

public static void printRev ( int[ ] data, int first, int last )

```
        6000
       ┌─────┬─────┬─────┬─────┐
       │ 74  │ 36  │ 87  │ 95  │
       └─────┴─────┴─────┴─────┘
       data[0] data[1] data[2] data[3]
```

The call
printRev ( data, 0, 3 );
should produce this output:    95  87  36  74

## Base Case and General Case

A base case may be a solution in terms of a "smaller" array. Certainly for an array with 0 elements, there is no more processing to do.

Now our general case needs to bring us closer to the base case situation. That is, the length of the array to be processed decreases by 1 with each recursive call. By printing one element in the general case, and also processing the smaller array, we will eventually reach the situation where 0 array elements are left to be processed.

In the general case, we could print either the first element, that is, data[first]. Or we could print the last element, that is, data[last]. Let's print data[last]. After we print data[last], we still need to print the remaining elements in reverse order.

## Using recursion with arrays

```
public static void printRev ( int [ ] data,        // Array to be printed
                              int first ,          // Index of first element
                              int last )           // Index of last element
// Result: Prints elements data [first] . . . data [last] in reverse order
{
    if ( first <= last )        // General case
    {
        outFile.print( data [ last ] + "  " );    // print last element
        printRev ( data, first, last - 1 ) ;      // then process the rest
    }
                                // Base case is empty else-clause
}
```

# Notes

## printRev(data, 0, 2) Execution

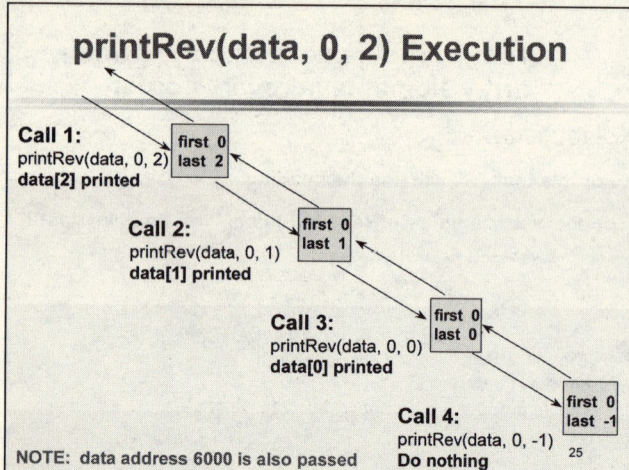

**Call 1:**
printRev(data, 0, 2)
**data[2] printed** — first 0, last 2

**Call 2:**
printRev(data, 0, 1)
**data[1] printed** — first 0, last 1

**Call 3:**
printRev(data, 0, 0)
**data[0] printed** — first 0, last 0

**Call 4:**
printRev(data, 0, -1)
**Do nothing** — first 0, last -1

NOTE: data address 6000 is also passed

---

## "Why use recursion?"

These examples could all have been written without recursion, by using iteration instead. The iterative solution uses a loop, and the recursive solution uses an if statement.

However, for certain problems the recursive solution is the most natural solution. This often occurs when structured variables are used.

---

## Recall that . . .

- Recursion occurs when a method calls itself (directly or indirectly).

- Recursion can be used in place of iteration (looping).

- Some algorithms can be written more easily using recursion.

**Notes**

## Recursion or Iteration?

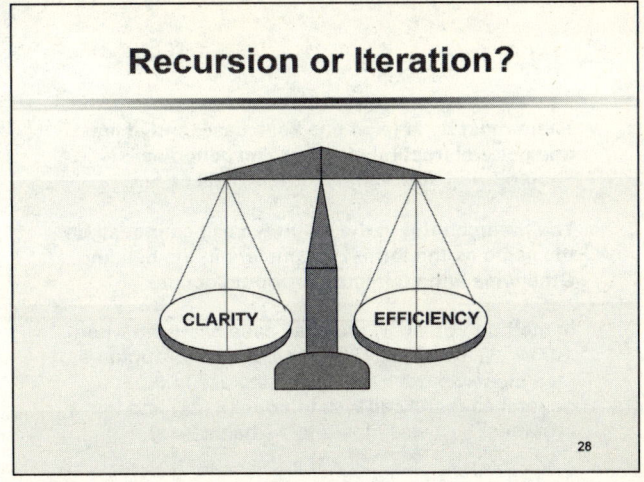

CLARITY    EFFICIENCY

## What is the value of `rose(25)`?

```
public static int rose ( int n )
{
        if ( n == 1 )          // Base case

              return 0;
        else                   // General case

              return ( 1 + rose ( n / 2 ) );
}
```

## Finding the value of `rose(25)`

```
  rose(25)                         the original call
= 1 + rose(12)                     first recursive call
= 1 + ( 1 + rose(6) )              second recursive call
= 1 + ( 1 + ( 1 + rose(3) ) )      third recursive call
= 1 + ( 1 + ( 1 + (1 + rose(1) ) ) )   fourth recursive call
= 1 + 1 + 1 + 1 + 0
= 4
```

## Writing recursive functions

- There must be at least one base case, and at least one general (recursive) case. The general case should bring you "closer" to the base case.

- The parameter(s) in the recursive call cannot all be the same as the formal parameters in the heading. Otherwise, infinite recursion would occur.

- In method `rose( )`, the base case occurred when `(n == 1)` was true. The general case brought us a step closer to the base case, because in the general case the call was to `rose(n/2)`, and the argument `n/2` was closer to 1 (than `n` was).

## When a method is called...

- A *transfer of control* occurs from the calling block to the code of the method. It is necessary that there be a return to the correct place in the calling block after the method code is executed. This correct place is called the *return address*.

- When any method is called, the *run-time stack* is used. On this stack is placed an *activation record* for the method call.

## Stack Activation Frames

- The *activation record* contains the return address for this method call, and also the parameters, and local variables, and space for the method's return value, if non-void.

- The activation record for a particular method call is *popped off the run-time stack* when the final closing brace in the method code is reached, or when a return statement is reached in the method code.

- At this time the method's return value, if non-void, is brought back to the calling block return address for use there.

# Notes

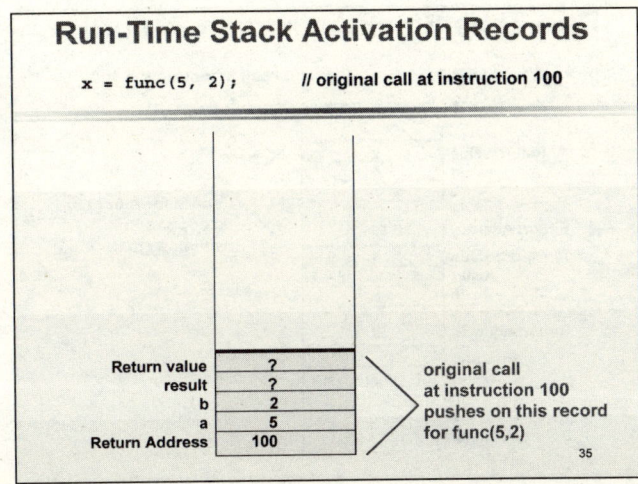
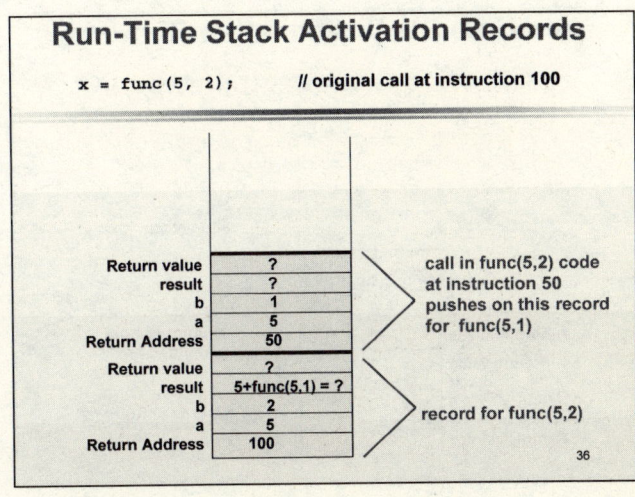

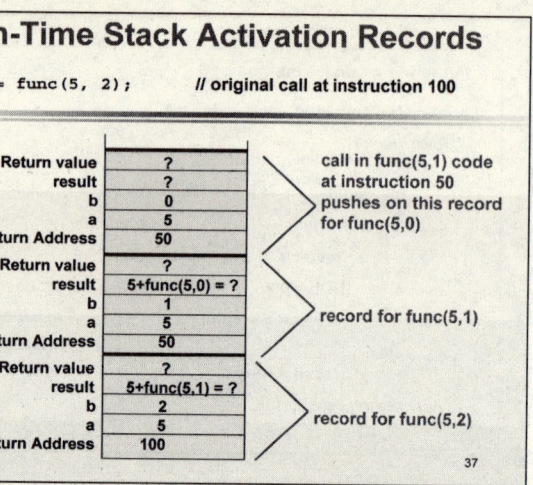

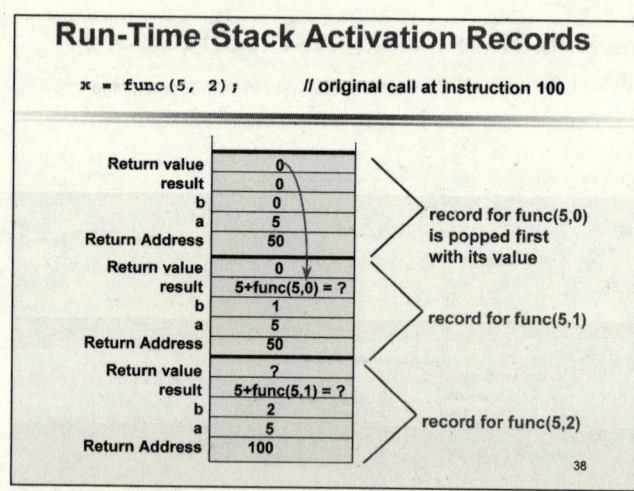

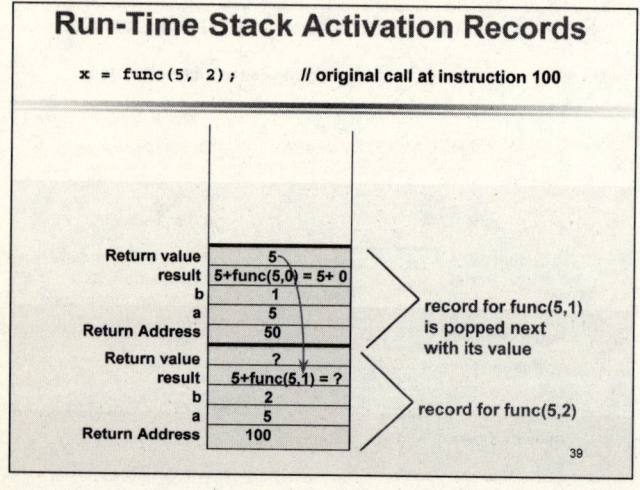

# Notes

## Run-Time Stack Activation Records

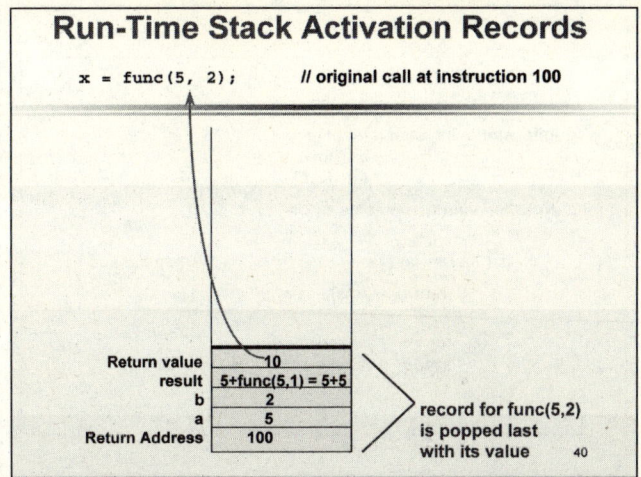

## Show Activation Records for these calls

x = func( -5, -3 );

x = func( 5, -3 );

What operation does func(a, b) simulate?

## Write a method . . .

- `sum` that takes an array `a` and two subscripts, `low` and `last` as parameters, and returns the sum of the elements `a[low] + . . . + a[last]`
- Write the method two ways -- using iteration and using recursion.
- For your recursive definition's base case, for what kind of array do you know the value of `sum(a, low, last)` right away?

```
// Recursive definition
public static int sum ( int [ ] a ,
                        int  low ,
                        int  last )
// Returns sum of elements a [low] . . . a [last]
{
        if ( low == last )              // Base case
                return a [low];

        else                            // General case
                return a [low] + sum( a, low + 1, last ) ;
}
```

## Write a method . . .

- **linearSearch** that takes an array `a` and two subscripts, `low` and `high`, and an `item` as parameters. Return true if `item` is found in the elements `a[low]...a[high]`. Otherwise, return false.

- Write the method using recursion.

- For your base case(s), for what kinds of arrays do you know the value of `linearSearch(a, low, high, item)` right away?

```
// Recursive sequential search
public static int linearSearch ( int [ ] a,   int  low,
                                 int  high, int  item )
// Returns true if item is in a [ low ] . . . a [ high ] ;
// false otherwise.
{
        if ( a [ low ] == item )         // First base case
                return true ;

        else if ( low == high)           // Second base case
                return false ;

        else                             // General case
                return linearSearch( a, low + 1, high, item ) ;
}
```

# Notes

## Array-based class `SortedList`

- isEmpty
- isFull
- length
- insert
- delete
- isThere
- resetList
- SortedList

Private data:
- numItems
- currentPos
- listItems [0]
  [1]
  [2]

## Binary Search in `SortedList`

- Examines the element in the middle of the array. Is it the sought item? If so, stop searching. Is the middle element too small? Then start looking in second half of array. Is the middle element too large? Then begin looking in first half of the array.

- Repeat the process in the half of the data that should be examined next.

- Stop when item is found, or when there is nowhere else to look and item has not been found.

## Binary Search Algorithm

- The Binary Search algorithm is, "Divide the list in half and decide which half to look in next. Division of the selected portion of the list is repeated until the item is found or it is determined that the item is not in the list."

- This algorithm is recursive!

## Recursive Binary Search

- The Binary Search algorithm can be written using iteration, or using recursion.

- `binIsThere` takes sorted array `listItems`, and two subscripts, `first` and `last`, and `item` as parameters. It returns true if `item` is found in the elements `listItems[first]...listItems[last]`. Otherwise, it returns false.

---

```
located = binIsThere( 0, 14, 25 );
                       first last item
```

subscripts

| 0 | 1 | 2 | 3 | 4 | 5 | 6 | 7 | 8 | 9 | 10 | 11 | 12 | 13 | 14 |
|---|---|---|---|---|---|---|---|---|---|----|----|----|----|----|
| 0 | 2 | 4 | 6 | 8 | 10 | 12 | (14) | 16 | 18 | 20 | 22 | 24 | 26 | 28 |

listItems

                              16  18  20  (22)  24  26  28

                                                24  (26)  28

                                                (24)

NOTE: ◯ denotes element examined

---

```
// Recursive definition
private boolean binIsThere ( int first, int last, int item )
//  Assumption:  List items are in ascending order
//  Returns   true if item is found in the list; false otherwise
{
    if ( first > last )              // Base case 1 -- not found
        return false;
    else
    {
        int mid ;
        mid = ( first + last ) / 2 ;
        if ( listItems [ mid ] == item )    // Base case 2 -- found at mid
            return true ;
        else if ( item < listItems [ mid ] )      // search lower half
            return binIsThere ( first, mid - 1, item );
        else                                       // search upper half
            return binIsThere ( mid + 1, last, item ) ;
    }
}
```

**Notes**

## Recursive Binary Search

- The recursive binary search function must be called from the `isThere` method of `SortedList` class.

```
public boolean isThere ( int item )
// Returns true if item is in the list; false otherwise.
// Assumption: List items are in ascending order
{
        return binIsThere ( 0, numValues - 1, item );
}
```

## Write a method . . .

- `minimum` that takes an array `a` and the `size` of the array as parameters, and returns the smallest element of the array. That is, it returns the smallest value of `a[0] ... a[size-1]`

- Write the method two ways -- using iteration and using recursion.

- For your recursive definition's base case, for what kind of array do you know the value of `minimum(a, size)` right away?

```
// Recursive definition
public static int minimum ( int [ ] a , int size )
// Returns smallest of a [ 0 ] . . . a [ size - 1 ]
{
        if ( size == 1 )                // Base case
            return a [ 0 ];
        else {                          // General case
            int y = minimum ( a, size - 1 );
            if ( y < a [size - 1] )
                return y ;
            else
                return a [ size -1 ] ;
        }
}
```